CRYING ALONE

Charleston, SC
www.PalmettoPublishing.com

Crying Alone
Copyright © 2021 by Bruce A. Jackson

First Edition

Hardcover ISBN: 978-1-64990-810-0
eBook ISBN: 978-1-64990-812-4
Paperback ISBN: 978-1-64990-813-1

Crying Alone

BRUCE A. JACKSON

CHAPTER #1

The Young Years

As a little boy, little did I know what lay ahead in my life. I was born in late May in northern Wisconsin. It was a small town called Rice Lake. A population of approximately 5,000 at the time and not many factories. Farming and lumbering were the largest industries in the area. There were several small companies and business in the area too. They also had a few stores, like the grocery store, an appliance store, and a small auto dealership on the main street.

As the youngest child, 1953 contained the earliest memories I had. Some of them were great, and others were not so good. It is funny how some memories stay with you all your life, and others disappear quickly.

Our family consisted of six in 1953. There was Mother Ethel, my sister Ferris, who was fifteen, Leo, who was fourteen, Karen, who was ten, Dennis, who was five. And me, Bruce, at three. Two of our family members were missing in my early life. My dad, Wallace, and my oldest brother, Douglas.

The earliest memories were of a family that struggled but were close through all the pain and changes. We would be torn in different directions over the next several years. The oldest and missing child of the family was Douglas. He was lost in the Korean War. I never knew him, I only knew him by the picture that hung on the wall. It also contained the medals he received.

Often Mother would take the picture of Douglas down from the wall. She would tremble and burst into tears. We would gather close around her during these trying times. It brought us to tears also as she fondly remembered her oldest son. He'd been killed a few years earlier in 1950 during intense fighting in Korea. It was also the year I was born. She would ask God, "Why? God? Why my dear son Douglas? Why?" The picture came down on several occasions. It just so happened that it was also the year my father had passed away. Douglas died at the age of seventeen. Somehow, he entered the service early at the age of sixteen and got pressed into service soon after training.

She not only wept for her oldest son but for a husband, who left her way too soon and unexpectedly. The heavy black makeup she wore would stream down her face, along with the tears. She would break down on many occasions.

Father was not here now because he had died shortly after his oldest son, Douglas, passed away. I never knew either of them but often missed them both in my tears for many years to come.

I was finally told several years later. Whenever I asked about my father, my close family members would say, "He passed away on your grandfather's farm in a terrible farm accident. "One of those large hooks that brings the straw and hay into the barn fell on him, and he died at the hospital."

That was the story, and I accepted it as the truth since it came from one of the close family members. Years later, I learned it was a good story to tell a small boy at the time. I was too young to know the truth and they did their best to shield me from it.

The story changed as I grew older; aunts and uncles would tell me a totally different story. They would say, "You are now old enough to know the truth about how your dad really passed away. So sorry, Bruce. He committed suicide earlier with a gun."

It would not be until I was twenty years old that I was able to pull all the pieces together and understand why he would do such a thing. Why certain circumstances would make him take his own life while he still had a family.

Growing up without him was difficult. I often wondered what he was like. What would it be like to even talk with him? I asked myself whether he would've liked me.

Father worked in a lumber yard for little pay. The work was very exhausting and hard. There was lots of heavy lifting and long hours. As far as I could tell, money was hard to come by, and my father lived paycheck to paycheck trying to take care of his large family. The pressure was so great, and losing his oldest son, whom he loved dearly, brought on even greater bouts of depression. He saw what it was doing to his wife, and he did not know how to deal with it. He sure did not have the money or resources to get help at that time.

Everyone said Dad was liked by so many. People loved him because he was so friendly and always had a big smile. A very outgoing gentlemen who lots of people knew. They only saw him from the outside and never the pain he held within him.

Soon after Douglas and Father were gone, Mom and the five of us tried to stay together. Mother struggled daily. There was never much food on the nearly empty shelves—and less in the refrigerator.

We were kids, so the outdoors were our relief from many of the sad things around us. Every day was an adventure. We would spend long hours together doing things. This story is as remembered from the youngest.

Monthly, Mother received a check from the government due to the loss of Douglas in the service. It helped but did not last long. We waited for it to arrive, and she was in her happiest moods when the mail man delivered it at the end of the month.

Some groceries, like bologna, bread, sugar, milk, and a few canned goods, would have to last us until that next check came. She took the rest and used it to purchase the liquor that helped her cope with her depression and problems.

Making do with what we had was always a challenge for us. We soon would be challenged regularly. No food in the cupboards and less money to get by.

Mother would soon be absent a great amount of time also from our little apartment. At first, for only a few hours at a time—but then a longer and longer time. Many hours passed, and then sometimes overnight. The reason soon became apparent. It was her way of attempting to deal with losing her husband and oldest son.

With no father around, Mother and the rest of us tried to stay together as best as we could. Not knowing what changes the future would bring for all of us.

It is one of these memories that came back like it was yesterday. I was jumping on a big bed to see if I could jump higher and higher each time. My little legs pushed hard after each jump. With each try, I could see the ceiling getting closer and closer. I held a nickel in my mouth that I had found outside. My belief was that it was in the safest place to keep it at the time. As I jumped higher, the nickel jumped up and down in my mouth. Somehow, the nickel got pressed to the roof of my mouth by my tongue. Soon, I realized that it was now stuck firmly there and I could not move it. I tried to release it but had no luck. Even my small finger did not do the trick. With tears now streaming from my eyes, I got off the bed and went running into the living room, where the rest of the family had gathered.

Leo, Karen, Ferris, and Dennis were there laughing at the time. My sister Karen asked, "Why are you crying?"

As I pointed to my mouth, she pulled me closer to her. Karen soon realized what the problem was from my pointing.

"The coin is stuck to the roof of his mouth!" she exclaimed.

Luckily, she had long enough fingernails to pry the nickel loose from its spot. I immediately stopped crying at her success. The rest of them laughed even more.

Leo, the second oldest, who had now taken over the role of the "man of the house" by then, felt it was his duty to scold me. He let me know to never put coins or other things in my mouth again. I knew he was serious from the tone of his voice. I now cried since I was the center of all the attention. I thought they were all laughing at me. Dennis wiped the tears from my face and tried to tell me it was going to be fine. After it was over, Mother kissed and hugged me. They laughed even more, since she left a large amount of the bright red lipstick on the side of my face. She now moistened her handkerchief with her tongue and rubbed the lipstick off my face.

Soon I was back on my bed, and the crying was over. Even though I'd done something wrong and was the center of unwanted attention, I knew it would be ok. I knew they loved me as I loved them.

We children spent more and more time outside. It would be even more when Mother was gone so much. We tried to do things together and with neighbor kids around us. Some black, some Spanish, but mostly poorer kids, just like us.

It was at these times I realized that a real family consisted of a father and mother. When other kids ran inside for dinner, they usually were together with a mother and father. They also had regular meals together. I did not know it at the time, but I was jealous of them and jealous of the nice meals they had. A Spanish family invited me in on several occasions to eat when I was done playing with their son. They must have known we did not eat much. I soon tried to visit them on a regular basis because I hoped to get some of the great food she made by hand.

Winter brought new problems to deal with, such as very few warm clothes and food. We were hungry often. Many times, I searched for something to eat in the cupboards. There was nothing much around. I learned that bread dipped in milk and cinnamon sprinkled on top was a treat if the pains got too great. Also finding a full can of corn after Leo sent me indoors was a real joy at the time. My brothers and sisters stayed outside in the snow, and I felt lucky at my find. I slowly peeled the can open with the opener and saw the bright yellow corn. With a dry piece of bread—this would be great for me.

I set the opened can on top of the stove. I then turned on the control for the electric stove to start. Quickly I ran outside again to join the others. They played a snow game, and I soon joined in. It was not long before Dennis and Leo were yelling, "Fire! Fire! The house is on fire!" We could all see the black smoke coming from around the windows. We ran upstairs to check it out. The can I'd placed on the stove had filled the room with black smoke. Leo grabbed it off the stove and turned the stove quickly off. Fortunately, the wall did not start burning. It was just the corn burning inside the can.

Leo was not happy, but he did remember telling me to go inside and find something to eat when I complained how hungry I was. He grabbed me by the neck and let me know to never touch that stove again. It took some time to clear the smoke from the room. I later hid under my bed covers so I would not get into trouble the rest of the night. I was still hungry at the time, hoping some food would come tomorrow.

It was then that Dennis had more trouble seeing things. His eyes were giving him problems. Mom brought into an eye doctor to get his eyes checked out. It was determined that he needed glasses urgently. When he returned home, I saw him for the first time with glasses on. It scared me, and I ran to my bedroom. After seeing him, I became emotional and pouting. I was sure he was going to die. This was not the same person to me. I thought something was deadly wrong or medically wrong with him and it might be life threatening. I did not want to lose him too. Soon I realized that it was very common for people to get glasses. He was not going to die, and I felt so much better the next day.

On several occasions, Mother would drive several miles away to Grandfather's farm. It was a small farm of about forty acres. It consisted of a barn, a machine shed, an outhouse, and the main house. It was a two-story house with a main bedroom downstairs and two bedrooms upstairs. It contained a kitchen, a living room, and storage area.

Mother would drive, and she would constantly be smoking as she did all day long. Her habit grew to three packs a day, but we got used to it. Grampa and Grandma would always be happy to see us and hug us. They were tight hugs, and I felt they would take away our breaths. The farm had no electricity, so the work was very difficult. All the cooking was done on an old cast-iron stove in the kitchen. Grampa always made sure there was enough wood close by on the floor. Grandma also pumped her water in the kitchen close to the old sink. I recall it was a small red-handled pump. The water was always refreshing and cold, straight from the well. She moved the black kettles back and forth from sink, stove, and oven.

It was also a time when outdoor toilets were common in the country. Many farmers had them since only city folks had indoor plumbing—or richer people had fancy indoor sinks, tubs, and toilets. Grandma and Grampa also had a large Sears catalog lying there inside on the floor. It was another thing we had to get used to using when we visited.

I often thought how difficult it must have been in the winter. Sometimes there were fifteen inches of fallen snow on the ground, and when it got to be twenty below zero, the wind chill made it even colder. Snow would pile high between the main house and the outhouse. It was a short walk of about fifty to seventy-five feet from the house, but I am sure it was always a fast walk.

Dennis, Karen, and I would sit in Grandma's white kitchen on the stair steps. They led upstairs to the other bedroom. Several heavy quilts were used in the long winter. We anxiously waited for the sugar cookies to be done in the oven. The room was always filled with that sweet smell. We knew to stay out of the way when Grandma was baking or cooking. There was not much room in the small kitchen.

Grampa and Gramma had no TV, radios, or record player for entertainment. Not even lights. When it started to get dark, they knew it was time to get ready for bed. The only entertainment they had was a big player piano in the living room. It had to be pumped with your feet. It gave us lots of fun together, and we enjoyed the time with Grandma and Grandpa. They had a large selection of rolls of music in a box nearby, you could pick out the one you wanted. All you had to do was start the paper slowly on a wooden roll. You then started pumping with your feet to make it work. It was always a challenge for us kids. The taller kids could work the pumps while sitting on the bench. It was fun to see the keys work and hear the music. We loved it, and our grandparents did too because they knew each song and they knew we were happy at the time.

They shoveled the coal in the stove daily to heat and cook. It was always a happy place to visit. They always made us feel welcome.

Mother left for the local watering hole or tavern, and we did not see much of her at these times. It was more often than we liked. Grandpa spent most of the time with us when we were there. He always told us he needed help from Dennis and me in the barn. He would exclaim, "We were the perfect guys to help him." If he were about to go out to the far field to get a new calf or if he needed help cleaning the manure from the barn, we were eager to be the helpers he needed.

It was a hilly little farm with corn, hay, and straw. He often helped the neighbors, and they helped him do the harvest when it was time in the fall. They all assisted one another.

Since there was no electricity, he had to milk the cows by hand. Early in the morning and about 5:00 p.m. in the evening. He milked about twelve cows by hand, so it was not easy to do. It took a few hours for him to finish. The milk went into large cans that had to be brought to town daily in his small pickup truck. The processing plant gathered milk from many farms daily. Most of farmers could not keep it cool long enough at the rural farms. If they kept it too long and it was warm, it would spoil.

Playing in the fields was always an adventure for us. They stacked the straw in large upright piles and in large rows. They were only fifty feet apart from each other in the rows. They would be picked up later by horse and wagon. We ran and hid behind the stacks and chased each other around the field. Usually several kids from the area joined us.

On occasion Dennis and I would go to see the cows when they were out in the fields. They seemed like dinosaurs to me since I was so small. When we went into the barn, I was sure they could kick me with those big, long legs. I carefully walked as near to the center of the walkway and as far from them as I could.

Grandpa always told us to stay away from the bull: "He can hurt you." We tried to get close to the cows in the field, but the bull prevented us from getting too close. He did a lot of loud snorting and scratching the ground. When he snorted at us, we knew it was dangerous and to stay far away.

As the cows were now at the bottom of the other side of the hill, we decided it was time for us to go back to the house. We wanted to see if we could get some of those great cookies Gramma was baking. We would race down the hill on the other side and see who was faster, Dennis or myself. It was agreed that the race would be run to the fence, where Grandpa was doing his repairs .

Off we went down the hill at full speed. I got the early lead, but Dennis soon caught up and passed me halfway down the hill. Our little legs went faster and faster.

As we got closer and closer to Grandpa, the race got closer and closer between us. Dennis must have kicked it in even harder as we came ever nearer to Grampa. Right before we got to the fence, Dennis slipped on a giant cow pie and fell forward. He then faceplanted in what must have been the largest cow pie in the whole field. He was now sliding quickly toward Grandpa.

"I won the race," Dennis said, but now Grandpa and I were laughing hard as I rolled in the grass. I could see the tears in Grandpa's eyes from laughing so hard. Dennis's face was covered with the mess, along with most of the front of him.

"Let's go to the house," Grampa chuckled, as we only had a short distance to go. He took us each by our hands and away we went. He wanted to show the rest in the house how we looked before we could get cleaned up. As we each entered the small two-story house, they all had a great laugh. Gramma told us to "Get out and get cleaned up before you come in here. Run some water on him." She always kept the house clean. Grandpa was still laughing as we turned to go outside once more.

I got picked to pump the water from the well. Up and down I struggled to pump the water; the pump was bigger than me. It lifted me off the ground on several occasions. When Grandpa pumped it for me, I got all wet. Grandpa told Dennis to put his head and face under the flow of cold water. It took a while, but he got all cleaned up and rinsed off. The hot sun dried both of us in our little shirts and pants. Soon we were back in the kitchen to eat the great meal Grandma and the girls had made.

The homemade apple pie was our reward for cleaning our plates, along with homemade ice cream. We had all took our turns spinning the beaters to make the ice cream by hand. It took some time, but we were overjoyed at our results.

Dennis and I learned that not far from Grandpa's farm was a large pond. We ventured there to check it out on several occasions. The first time will always stick with me because of the lesson I learned while there.

We were sure that it was deep enough to float across since we were not able to swim yet. We each found a log to sit on. We splashed around at the outer edge of the pond. Going deeper, I sat on the log and told Dennis I was floating. I should have been watching him more closely, but I paid little attention to him since I was having so much fun.

He soon snuck up behind me and give me a big push while I sat on the log. I was now really floating toward the center of the pond. The fear started to overcome me. I heard him laughing as I floated away from him, closer and closer to the center of the pond. I started to cry because of the fear of the unknown and how deep it must've been.

As I drifted farther away, I yelled and waved my arms, but it was no help. Soon I fell into the water, splashing about in fear. To my surprise, the water was not deep at all. Only a foot or two up to my chest. I stood right up and yelled at him for doing what he did. He laughed even more now because he'd known how deep it really was before we got there.

We spent hours there crossing the pond over and over. I learned how to swim on Grampa's farm after several visits. Discovering many things and learning daily, we loved it each time we visited.

Grandpa and Grandma both processed the food they needed for staying on the farm. The basement revealed row after row of vegetables, corn, beans, carrots, beets, tomatoes, potatoes, and even meat in jars. Grampa also made his own root beer, which was always a treat for us. Rows of hanging onions and other things in the cool basement kept them fed well through the winter. Nuts of different kinds, like walnuts, acorns, and almonds in bags, also could be found down there. Summer brought large amounts of strawberries, apples, raspberries, and sweetcorn from Grandmas large garden. Grandma and the girls made several jams of strawberries, apples, and raspberries.

Grandmother, along with Karen and Ferris, would spend time in the kitchen making pies, cakes, and cookies or getting ready for the next meal. If not there, they spent a lot of time in the garden. When they were not in the kitchen or garden, they would try to spend time with Dennis and me outside. Mother seemed to be gone a lot of the time. She would show up later in the evening. The smell of alcohol was common when she got close. Grandmother always seemed to convince her to rest or go to bed when she came in. Her slurred speech was obvious, and we hoped she would not break down again and start crying about her losses .Sometimes she would pull Dennis and me close to her and tell us how much she cared for us. It was always an emotional time.

We moved on several occasions. Possibly because of the constant late rent or because we were thrown out. She may have just not paid rent at all. She may have used the money for her habit. We never knew when we were moving next.

Dennis had his ways of pulling tricks on his younger brother on several occasions. We played in the fields and open yards close to our house. After a while, we heard Leo or Karen calling for us to come in and eat, and we came as fast as we could. On one occasion, Dennis and I climbed on top of a couple of fence posts at the farm next door, which was close to our yard. The grass was high, and the fences were not kept up since the farm next to us had been abandoned for many, many years.

As we started to climb down from the tall fence posts, Dennis yelled, "Snake! Snake!" He said it was near the bottom of my post and not to get down or it would get me. "It is huge," he exclaimed, and I quickly got back up to the top as fast as I could. I was sure it was there and ready to strike or wrap me up, even though I could not see it. Dennis moved closer to the house and yelled again for me not to get down: "It's real close to you!" he shouted. "It could eat you!"

I believed him because he always protected me.

Now, I was scared as could be; time was passing quickly. Surely this snake was going to climb up that post to get me. Now alone and in tears, I could tell it was getting darker and darker outside.

The house was close enough that I could hear the others now laughing in it as I wished I could be close to them. I thought I was going to miss something to eat also. Soon, Leo appeared out the back door of the house. He walked toward me, laughing as he got closer.

"Get down, Bruce!" he yelled. "There is no snake there. Your brother is just pulling a trick on you."

It was not until Leo got close to me that I was ready to get down from that post. He reached out for me and grabbed my arms. I was still shaking, so it was a struggle to get me off the post as I clung tight. Once he had me, I held on tight with my legs wrapped around him.

Leo carried me as we reached the house. They all had big laughs at how Dennis had convinced me about the snake at the bottom of my post. Dennis would remind even years down the road.

We spent most of our young lives doing everything together. Being only a year and a half older than me, he always watched out for me, and when it got too hard to handle, I cried out for my father. He even hugged me to comfort me in the pain. It would happen on several occasions in the upcoming years, especially after we were torn from the family.

At one location, we soon learned that the local junkyard was not too far from our house. The local kids told us to be very careful when getting close to the junkyard. We were told it was run by the Devil himself. The Devil Man ran it. The man that worked there was a big man, always looking to spear some kids, we were told. For some reason, that statement scared us but made us want to go and check it out even more.

The local kids we became friends with decided it was time we should see the "The Devil Man" for ourselves. We would venture out tomorrow. I recall lying in bed the night before, my eyes wide open, wondering what this guy looked like. Was he really this close to us? Was he straight from hell? Would he have horns too?

The next day came and Dennis and I and two of our friends decided we had to go and check this junkyard out. We knew we would have to sneak up on the "Devil Man" and make sure we got back home safely. No one was going to stop us now. We agreed to not tell anyone of our plans or some adult or someone would try to stop us. We were going on this journey one way or another.

We got close to the junkyard, crawling the last fifty feet on our bellies in the high grass. We moved slowly on our hands and knees. The edge was now near as we saw black smoke swirling in the air from trash burning below in a large pit about twenty feet deep and several hundreds of feet across.

Peering over the edge of the junkyard, I could now see the man that the other older kids had told us about. He was a tall, thin, black man. He had the fork they mentioned to keep the trash burning by continually stirring it. Our two new friends told us to slowly get as close as we could. We would start throwing what we could toward the so-called "Devil Man" to keep him as far from us as we could. We also needed to stay far away from that terrible fork that he threatened to use on us.

The tossing of cans and junk started as soon we got over of the edge. We went onto the trash that was dumped over the edge from the residents in the area. Closer and closer we got, tossing trash as hard as we could toward the "Devil Man." The smell was tremendous, and seeing a rat or two did not help. I was now as scared as I could be. I wondered if the "Devil Man" could reach me now with that long fork.

Slowly he turned toward us, and I heard the anger in his voice. "You kids better run! he yelled. The fork was now being raised high in the air. I was sure he was going to throw it my way. I turned around as fast as my little body would turn. The other three boys were already running halfway up the trash heap, scrambling to the edge of the dump, trying to get away now. "Run! Run! Save yourself!" I heard. Now I could not go fast enough. I was sure the "Devil Man" was going to get me next. I was sure that his spear was going to reach me and hurt so much. Could I save myself?

Making it to the upper edge of the trash, I frantically reached for the grass on top to pull myself over the edge. I felt I could get away safely. I could no longer see my brother or friends. They were far ahead of me now.

Soon I was on top, and I could hear the others still yelling frantically for me to hurry: "Don't let him get you!" They were already far ahead of me when I finally stood up to run.

Scared to even turn around to see how close the "Devil Man" was to me, I started to run fast trying to save myself, I was confident I could get home safely if my legs could move fast enough. With lots of trash around the edge of the dump too, I quickly tripped and fell on my belly. As fate would have it, a broken beer bottle lay right were my knee landed, cutting it wide open. The cut was quite large, and I now started to bleed a lot. As it trickled down my leg, I could see it was now flowing into my tennis shoe.

The house was probably only a block or two away, but it seemed like miles to me. I ran into the house, yelling for my sister, mother, or someone to help me. Mother soon appeared and asked what I was yelling about. She quickly saw the stream of blood flowing down my leg and pulled me into the bathroom to clean it up. It seemed big at the time, but it probably wasn't in retrospect.

She searched for bandages and some type of wrapping for my knee but with no luck. Then she went to the drawer in the kitchen and came back with a large roll of black electrician's tape.

Around and around my knee, she wrapped the tape to stop the bleeding and close the cut. After several minutes, I could see she had wrapped it more than enough. She had tears in her eyes as she told me never to go over there again. I tried to stand and bend my knee but with little luck. I told her that I had gotten away from the "Devil Man" and that I was ok. She held me close for an usually long time.

My friends asked often what had happened to me because they saw the big black tape job on my leg. I soon wore it with pride as I explained to them that I'd gotten away from the "Devil Man," but it was really close.

Later I learned that the man that managed the dump was just doing his job. He continued to yell and scare kids away so they would not get hurt in the junkyard. It was no place for us to play. We would tell the story of the "Devil Man" to younger kids that came to our neighborhood. It was like a rite of passage for all us.

———

Mother took Dennis and me along with her as she visited the many bars around home and in the area. Many times, I woke up in the back seat of the car between midnight and five in the morning. Sometimes I would wake up, and she would be passed out in the front seat. The sun shining bright. Other times she would wake us up to go home when she was with a stranger. The colorful neon lights in the windows and front doors were always inviting to those who searched them out.

If she came home and we were waiting for her, often I was sleeping on the couch or in a chair in the living room. When she brought men home, they scared me since I did not know them.

One guy especially scared me , his name was Elno. He was a big man who smelled bad and was always drunk along with Mom. Worse, he had one eye that looked one way, and the other looked off into the other direction. He had a foul mouth, and I recall he treated my mother nasty. If Leo was sleeping or not there, he felt he could take advantage of her. I saw too much as a young boy. His hands all over her and pulling her cloths from her. She got slapped around more as the drinking got worse and worse.

Upon entering the upper apartment, they staggered in, and I waited on the big-cushioned chair. Fear now overtook me. He yelled a few obscenities at her and turned to sit. Before I could get out of the chair, he sat squarely right on top of me. I cried out for help. The weight was painful. I must have been there several minutes before heard the bedroom door open. Thankfully, it was Leo; he must have herd the cries. He ran over to me at the chair and started to pull Elno off of me. Elmo must have thought it was ok to swear at Leo too, but that was a mistake in his drunken condition.

Leo started to punch him about the head while trying to free me. Soon Elno was laying on the floor, and Leo was kicking him. He told him to keep his mouth shut: "Don't ever talk to my mom like that again either." The memory of this night would not last long for him—but a lifetime for me.

Thanksgiving night came in November, and the girls, Ferris and Karen, eagerly waited for Mom to come home from the local bar. They had done what they could to make a nice meal for all of us. Saving a few items for this occasion and borrowing a few others from the neighbors, they had the table set, expecting Mother at the house by 7:00 p.m., as she had instructed them. . Mother never showed up, and we all anxiously waited for her to arrive, peering out the windows for several hours. I recall the girls had buns made, a fat turkey in the oven, cranberries, along with the stuffing and potatoes. Even a big apple pie sat on the table. They were eager to show mom. I never remember the house smelling better. We were so excited. The girls were so proud to show Mother what they had accomplished together.

The time passed, and it got later and later. It was now about 11:00 p.m. when the car lights appeared in the driveway. Stll the girls were anxious to show Mother what they'd done to make this a nice Thanksgiving dinner. Dennis woke me up to help surprise Mother as they came up the stairs. Leo was now gone, and the four of us stood near the door as it opened. In she came, and we could see she was having trouble with Elmo. Her tears were apparent, and she quickly went to the bathroom to try and get the swelling down on her face. Elmo entered with obscenities for all of us. The girls did not know what to say, and neither did we boys.

As soon as he saw how the table was set and what the girls had done, his swearing had the girls in tears in a very short time. He started to knock things off the table in his drunken state. He then went directly for the turkey the girls had set on the table.

Grabbing the turkey off the table, he quickly went to the window. Opening with one hand and holding the turkey in the other, out the window he threw it, dropping it two stories to the trash heap below. I saw it tossed and knew we would have no turkey dinner tonight. I also knew that, if it went out that window, there was only junk and trash between our house and the one next door. The houses were very close, and trash built up in between them. I also knew that I had seen rats and mice among the trash down there on more than one occasion. Once a rat had skittered across my arm, my reflex was to grab it away and try to keep it from biting me. I got a hold of the tail and started swirling it around and around in the air. It was a short time, and all I had in my palm was a long tail . Scared, I tossed it as far as I could.

This night was over in a hurry. We all cried as we found our places to sleep. The next morning, our mother tried to comfort the girls with little luck. Elno was nowhere to be seen. This would not be the last time we would have trouble with him. She brought him home often, and the conflicts unfortunately continued.

As Leo got older, he got stronger and more protective of us when Elmo was around. On one occasion, Leo must have told him to stay away, and he showed up anyway, drunk with Mother. Elmo took a swing at her, and Leo was on top of him right away. Leo chased him around the kitchen table with a bat letting him know he was going to pound him silly. Around the table they went until Elmo was finally caught. After a few blows, Elmo was out the door and down the steps outside with Leo still after him again.

As the chase continued outside and around the car, we watched out the window and all laughed as Leo did his best to teach him a lesson. Several different men came and went over the next several years. We never did welcome them very much because we knew they were not our real father. I did not see Elmo much after that. Big changes were about to happen to our little group.

Mother took Dennis and me along to the bars with her on many occasions. Dennis and I continued to be close even as we grew older. We soon learned that, when she took us with her, we could get change from the customers in the bar. We would tell them we could really jig or dance. Most of them would give us a dime or quarter just to see what we could do. We would jump around and act like we knew what we were doing. We made enough to buy chips, candy, and soda. We jigged a lot, and sometimes until we got so tired, we had to go to the car to rest up or sleep. It was not unusual that some weeks we would go to the bar several times.

It was not uncommon to wake up in the morning and still be in the same bar. We slept with Mother in the car.

Very often we found no food in the house. We learned, if we had bread in the house, we could soak it in milk or water to make a meal. Milk and a little cinnamon on bread could easily be a meal—not to mention how lucky we felt if we had some corn-flakes to soak in water if no milk was available.

Neighbor kids who were Spanish were now a possibility for food. I learned to play with them, and when they had to be home to eat, I would follow them home. Often, I was invited in, and I was introduced to an all-new kind of food. Handmade food that was scrumptious. I would go home after I'd had my fill and brag to my brothers and sisters about how good the food was.

CHAPTER #2

Moving Again

We soon moved to a suburb on the west side of Milwaukee, West Allis, Wisconsin. It was a totally different world for us compared to the several small towns in northern Wisconsin. It was busy, with lots of people and traffic like I had never seen. It was so very different than the country living we were used to. It was a small upstairs apartment. With my little legs it was all I could do to go up and down the steps. The stairs would wind around and down to the busy streets below.

I would admire the many kinds of cars that passed our upper apartment. Counting them was difficult since there were so many.

Now the sounds of traffic came up to our windows, along with the cries of street vendors. Weekly one of the vendors would push his cart down the street and announce that he had fruits and vegetables available for sale. "Bananas, onions, corn, beans, watermelons!" he would shout out so all could hear in the area.

Mother would sometimes give me a dollar and send me downstairs and out to the street to get some corn or melons. Other times she would give me the dollar to go and get her a few packs of cigarettes. It was easier to do at that time. I just told them it was for my mother. The grocery store owner never questioned me. Her habit now grew to three packs a day. It always seemed to me she had a cigarette burning, even when she was making something to eat. The Chesterfield Straits brand was popular at the time and had no filters.

Dennis and I would spend hours outside with neighbor kids or just trying to find something to do. Fortunately, we were only a few houses away from the auto repair shop and salvage yard. It was my introduction to an all-new world of interest that would last my entire life, the automobiles.

The fence around the yard was not much of a deterrent for us kids in the neighborhood. It soon became another playground for us to visit on a regular weekly and daily basis. That was until the owners acquired a big German shepherd dog to patrol the yard. We still got into the yard, but we made sure there was always an escape route for getting out quickly.

Sitting inside of the yard were 1920s, 1930s, and 1940s wrecks. Many were piled on top of one another. They were totally exciting for me. We sneaked inside the fence often. We would open the big old doors on the cars. We played with all the knobs on the dashboards and hopped from car to car. We pumped the floor pedals if we could reach them. Row after row of cars. Several acres invited us into this huge auto junk yard. We jumped on the running boards and slid down the backs of what seemed like big whales as we played. I even loved the smell of the musty old cars, pretending to race down the road or track in my mind.

CHAPTER # 3

A Scary Place

Miss Makins tried to assure us everything was going to be fine. "Are we coming back later?" I pleaded, but no response came back. Karen and Dennis were now silent as we moved down the road. I screamed as I saw Mother, Ferris, and Leo fade away as we got farther and farther down the street. I could not understand why we were being taken away.

It wasn't long before we arrived at the County Children's Home, a huge facility with several large buildings sitting on many acres on the west side of the large city of Milwaukee.

Karen was dropped off at a building away from the main facility where we were located. I later learned that it was a separate building for girls only and not the boys area. Dennis and I sat in the car as we waited for Miss Makins to return from bringing Karen to the proper girls living area. Now it was our turn. We now would be brought to the young boys area.

She returned to the main large building, where a big lady met us at the front door. I was scared now, especially of this huge place and more of this strange big lady. I now started to shake in fear. At the time, I was about six, and I knew I was supposed to be at home with my mother and family. This was not the place I was supposed to be. In we went, and Miss Makins slowly made her exit. Shortly after we were delivered to the big lady along with a file of papers on each of us, I saw the name tag on the big lady, and it read Mrs. Johnston. Even seeing the nice lady leave us here made me feel sick and scared at the time.

Now the lady—or "matron" as they were called back then—took us inside. She quickly changed her tone from being welcoming to a stern commanding voice. This transformation was somehow very normal for her. I sensed immediately that she did not like either one of us.

I now broke down crying and asked, "Where is my sister, Karen? Where is my mother?" And I ran toward the door. She ran after me and grabbed my arm and pulled me back. She squeezed my arm tightly and told Dennis and me to walk close to her as she walked down the hall. I sobbed as we were pulled along. We now were supposed to stay very close to her. She told us, "This is your new home! You will be living here. And don't cry for your mamma. They're not coming to get you either!"

She showed us to the clothing room to get our uniforms. We were to get rid of those clothes that we were wearing when we arrived. Soon her huge hands and fingers grabbed clothes from the different shelves. She told us to get our own cloths off right away and put on the little uniforms she tossed our way. The set consisted of a plain pea-green t-shirt, a pair of underwear, a small pair of bib overalls, a pair of dark-brown socks, and a worn pair of plain, brown shoes.

Next, we were shown down the stairs to where we would eat. It was a large room, and it was where the dining hall was. It was a big rectangular room of at least twenty circular tables. Each table was set with a white tablecloth and eight places for each of the kids to eat the next meal.

I could hear the boys from upstairs, and it sounded like a lot of them to me. Next, we were brought to one of the sleeping rooms. It was a very long, rectangular, open room with easily thirty beds on each side and a wide main isle down the middle of the floor. Two floor levels were just like this. And then it was onto the bathroom with several toilets, ten sinks, and about a dozen bathtubs. She informed us that baths were done on Saturday evenings and we were required to wash up good before each meal at the sinks. "Keep quiet or you don't eat."

With the tour over, she quickly brought us to where all the noise was coming from. It was the TV room. It had rows and rows of little wooden chairs. Lots of boys all sitting in neat straight rows watching *The Mickey Mouse Club*, *Roy Rogers*, and other kids shows. With only a few open chairs, Dennis and I were instructed to go and sit down.

"Sit and be quiet!" she said gruffly, and we did. Each of the boys was just like us, it seemed. They wore the exact same outfit we had just put on. We all looked exactly like one another, and we were all about the same age, three years old to ten years old.

The call to eat came soon enough, and we were instructed to line up to eat and, above all, to keep quiet. Still scared, I lined up like the rest as tears rolled down my face. Dennis was not far from me. We quietly marched to the dining room and filled one table at a time. No rushing around here, or you would have your ears grabbed or hair pulled by one of the matrons. They were instructed to maintain strict order.

That night came, and we were assigned beds to use while we were staying there. Not knowing how long we were going to be there, I cried, "Where is my family? Where are my aunts or uncles? Why was I left here? Why don't they come and get me?"

No response ever came. Where were Grampa and Grandma, I wondered. Time went on and on with no contact at all. The matrons for the night shift sat at the end of the large bed filled rooms. If it got noisy or she heard you talking to a boy next to you, she was at your bedside in a hurry with a long wooden paddle. A few whacks with that, and you kept quiet. The worst was still to come at this place, and I quickly learned to hate and fear it.

We saw that she kept a clip board with her while on duty. Before she left in the morning, she would hand it to the new matron coming on duty. You did not want your name on her clip board, or there would be hell to pay, as I found out early on.

Saturday came, and it was now time to get a bath right after breakfast. We lined up in rows at the bathtub room, waiting for our turn. With a dozen tubs, six had boys in, and six were emptying or filling with water for the next six kids. The matron moved methodically from tub to another tub to scrub us up quickly, only stopping to check her clipboard on occasion. You could tell she had an agenda to discipline those that she felt needed it. Especially if your name was on her clipboard.

Getting close to the bathing room, I heard the cries and screams of boys inside and some leaving the room. Now scared beyond belief, I feared getting closer and closer to the tubs. Soon I got to the front of the line, and I was the next one to get a tub; the matron called out my name. She now checked her clip board to see if my name was listed on it. Thank God it was not, but the boy behind me was, and he knew something bad was about to happen. Immediately he tried to pull away from her, crying at first then screaming, "No! No! Please!"

She grabbed him as he stood next to the tub filling with water. Into the water, she lifted him. She proceeded to shove his face and head under the water over and over. "You are not going to wet your bed again, are you?" she shouted.

"No! No!" he cried, and down into the water he went again, gasping for his next breath.

Now I realized what the clip board was used for and why the matrons went down the row of beds each morning. They quickly were putting their hands under the sheets as they made their inspections, and they checked to see if they were wet. Down one row and then up the other, looking for wet beds. Writing names down as they moved along.

After a few weeks of this terror , I woke up in the middle of the night. To my shock, I felt my own bed, and it was wet. Now frightened, I felt it would be my turn to end up on that list of names. Would I be listed to get punished for wetting my bed? Would I be one of those boys who got their heads dunked up and down in the tub? Slowly I slipped out of bed so the matron would not see me as she read her book. I peered over the side of the bed, watching her closely. She was toward the far end of the row of beds and reading her book. I knew I had to do something about this before morning. I knew that was the time when they checked all the beds to see if they were wet.

I peeled back the covers carefully and raised the sheet just high enough to get an air pocket under it. I then let it out again. For several hours, over and over I did this until I could not feel a wet spot in the middle of the bed. I pumped the air in and out.

Morning came, and I waited for the instructions for all of us to get out of our beds.

Down the row, the matron came, putting her hand under cover after cover. She got to my bed and kept on going down the row. I now felt a great relief. Fortunately, it was also the day to put on clean sheets. I felt I had just escaped the executioner. This must never happen again, I told myself, and fortunately it did not.

Time spent at the children's home was like being in a military school. Standing in rows, watching TV in rows, going to eat in rows, and moving about the facility in tight rows. Each of us in identical uniforms. Even going outside in the winter, you had to be in one of two rows with your sled on the hill. You held your sled in front of you at the top .If you got out of line, you were told to go to the back end. "Next! Next! Next!" was the yell of the matron if you made it to the front of the line. Down the hill you went after each kid ahead of you. "Next!" You went, sliding down the same grooves to the bottom and returning to the top.

When we arrived at the children's home, it was the first time I had seen black boys, and I soon became friends with several in the play yard. One became close; his name was Carl, and he had an infectious laugh that you always wanted to hear. The call for dinner came after playing outside, and I missed my new friend. I was sure I would see him inside or later. I always wanted to sit next to him because he was so friendly.

As we marched down the hallway toward the dining room, I heard someone crying and kicking, I thought, in the hallway. As I got closer to the noise, I could tell it was just behind the door to the clothing room. I quickly opened the door, and there was my friend Carl, hanging on a hook behind the door up in the air. He was kicking hard and crying. The tears ran down his face. The matron had picked him up by his shirt and overalls and hung him up there on the hook. She was standing there in front of him, yelling, "You're going to learn to keep your mouth shut, aren't you?" And he cried even harder kicking the door, unable to get himself down.

She quickly pushed me back out of the doorway and said I was next if I caused any trouble. I moved on down the hallway toward the dining room, but I could hear his cries for some distance as I moved on down the hallway. I learned it was a common practice to put kids on the door hook if the matrons felt they were a problem. I saw it several times.

Christmas was unusual to me since I had never experienced how they handled it here. A group of about twenty of us were brought into a larger room and were told to sit on the floor. We were reminded to be very quiet because Santa was going to arrive soon. We would listen very closely for his bells as he got closer and closer to our room.

The ringing started, and the excitement was peaking. "Santa's coming, and maybe he will have presents," we were told.

In came the fat man with his red and white outfit, shaking his band of bells. He dragged a huge bag with presents behind him. He asked us the usual questions, like "Have you all been good little boys?" and "Are you behaving here?" and "Are you eating all your vegetables and cleaning your plates?"

We all yelled, "Yes, Santa!" in unison with hopes he had something for each of us in his large white bag. He then took out the presents one at a time. Passing them out, making sure no one was forgotten. Bursting with excitement ,we opened the presents quickly and as fast as little kids could. Each kid getting one present.

I immediately noticed that there were three different kinds of presents in all the presents handed out. Each kid opened one of three boxes. It would be a pair of mittens, a stocking cap, or a large scarf. One only, and you could see that several in the room had the same present as you did.

As Santa left the room, he shook the bells hard and said he would see us next year. He would get ready for the next group of fifteen boys to enter the room after our group shuffled out.

When it was over, we were all brought to the clothing or coat room. Each kid brought what he had received. We were told to place our presents on the shelf in the proper area. We were to put them on the scarf shelf, the mittens shelf, or the hat shelf, for all the kids to use. They were not at all our personal presents. We all soon realized we were to give them up. They were for all the kids. It affected all the boys. Several cried as they were forced to give up their presents and put them on the correct shelf. For lots of the boys, this was the only present they would receive this Christmas. Most never saw a relative or family even during the holidays. That was true for us also.

Kids did not speak out of turn or say something the matrons did not like either. Dennis quickly learned this one time in the narrow hallway. He was instructed to move along in an orderly manner and to be quiet.

"You are not my mother or father," he let the matron know. The matron quickly reacted to what she called his smart mouth. She reached out and grabbed him on both sides of the head. She firmly grabbed him by the ears and started to raise him up in the air. I recall it precisely, since I was near him at the time. When his feet were off the ground, she started banging his head hard against the wall. "You won't smart off again, will you?" He got his head banged several times. I think it hurt me more than Dennis because, through my tears and trembling, I could see him get red and very quiet now. I could also see how scared he was. We've spoken of this for years since our time spent there.

The time we spent in the TV room had other purposes also. It also served as a viewing room for those people coming in to observe us boys. The people would try and pick one out or maybe two to bring to their home for a while. Possibly even start the foster child process. It was an ongoing process.

Imagine, if you will, a room full of boys, and we saw new people behind a large glass window watching us. Each of us knew why they were looking through the glass window. We quickly all raised up our hands and yelled out, "Take me! Take me! Take me!" We were like sheep being shown at an auction. Hoping someone would take us away from this terrible place, each of us scared in our own way. Always clinging to the possibility that my mother would come to get us or some relative would—but it never happened. Never again would our whole family be together again.

My oldest sister, Ferris, came once to visit us at the children's home, along with Leo. She soon moved out of the house and planned to go far away. We would spend a few years here at the children's home. Each worse than the next. Leo was ready to go into the army, and Ferris was off to California.

I had made several friends during the time we spent here. Playing outside around the many buildings. It was a time when we played marbles in the dirt because marbles were easily available. They were a very popular pastime. They were available in small bags located in cereal boxes, hobby shops, grocery stores, and more. Some came in a bag of about twenty pieces for only a few cents. Marbles could be acquired at the local hobby store or department store toy area. They even got them at gas stations. Many of the kids at the home had their parents bring them in when they visited. At least those boys who were lucky enough to have family visit.

My brother Dennis became somewhat known as the marble expert in the children's home. He played all the time in the yard. Many boys challenged him daily, trying to win his large amount of marbles. Each match was for the total amount put out to play in a large circle of dirt. It was always a battle to the finish. Soon he had several shoe boxes full. He also had several large bags of marbles he had won from each of the contestants. Marbles of every color and size. Cat's eyes, plain ones, steelies, and many others where in his collection, including the large and small. Several kids challenged him and lost large amounts of marbles.

Occasionally a fight broke out between two of the boys. It never lasted long, and each was sent to his bed. Missing supper was not unusual, and you'd better be really quiet while you were lying on your bed.

When it was time to go to sleep, all were instructed to kneel at the end of our beds for bedtime prayers. "Now I lay me down to sleep," could be heard in unison no matter what you were used to saying at home. Once the prayer was over, we were instructed to "get under the covers!" and turn the lights out. The only light seen was a dim, small one at the end of the room, where the night matron sat and read her books or papers.

People came to the TV room many times, and I saw kids leave time and time again.

Some years passed by, and finally we were told to go get cleaned up and get ready to go for a car ride again. Miss Makins was going to take us for a ride, and we knew something exciting was happening. We were told that someone was interested in possibly having us for the weekend. I did not know it at the time, but it was a trial weekend to see how it would work out or an introductory meeting. We then went back to the children's home until they decided if they wanted to go ahead and take us both in for a longer period of time as foster kids.

CHAPTER # 4

Finding A Family

Placing two boys instead of one was always more difficult to do for the county. Soon we went to a family in Muskego, Wisconsin. Dennis and I were kept together. Karen went on to another foster home in Milwaukee County. This new family of ours was a small family. They had one daughter, and we lived on a nice little lake. It was on the west side of Milwaukee, which was called Little Muskego Lake. It was the Bangle family. We learned how to water ski and attended a regular grade school. Never seeing any of our real family and wondering where they all were. I knew they were out there somewhere.

The year passed quickly, and Mrs. Bangle called to have Miss Makins come back and pick us up again. It was because she was pregnant and did not have the room to care for us any longer. It could have been the challenge of two little rascals too. It lasted through 1959. In the spring of 1960, we were on the move again. Many times, I wondered why Mother never picked us up or why any aunts or uncles never came to take us back home.

Fear of going back to the children's home came to me nightly.

We proceeded to return to the children's home but only for a few weeks.

Finally, it was time to say goodbye to the County Children's Home after more than three plus years. The place scared me when I arrived, and it scared me for years to come. Even when I passed by it as an adult, it brought back terrible memories. Sometime in the sixties, it was shut down as a children's home was converted to county offices and grounds. It was all remodeled and updated.

We then moved in with a family that would be our final foster home. Their names were Ervin and Mildred Saueressig. They would be the family we would finish grade school and high school with. They became Grandpa and Gramma to each of our children. They lived on a large farm outside of a small town called Batavia, Wisconsin. It was a German family that lived in the community for many years. His father had farmed in the area, and now Ervin did too. They had over two hundred acres, and it would be like our new giant playground.

The first visit had us checking out every part of the farm. We explored each of the sheds and the big barn full of animals. Pen after pen with rows of calves and young livestock. There were many cats, a beautiful collie, and much more. We ran out to the big field that held the cows. We wanted to check them out too. They usually kept one hundred to one hundred fifty cows on the farm. The milk house was modern and up to date with the latest equipment to milk cows. Lots of stainless steel. The newest invention for farms at that time was a glass pipeline, which drew visitors from all over the county. It got to be common to have visitors come when we milked sixty to seventy cows daily. They watched the milk run through the glass tubes to the milk house.

It was a great fascination to watch how it operated and pumped and dumped it into a large cooling tank in the milk house. After that, a big milk truck from the Bordens processing plant came and picked up the milk daily.

I was amazed at the large silos that stood near the barn. Three side by side, full of silage from the previous summer and fall. I immediately wanted to climb to the top as Miss Makins and the Saueressig family discussed the details of our visit in the house.

When they finally came outside, I was standing on the small, ten-inch edge at the top of the silo. They looked so small and seemed so far away. I yelled, "Hey, I'm up here," and I waved my arms. I struggled to keep my balance as the wind blew in my face.

They yelled back, "Get down right now!"

I could tell how scared they were as they rushed close to the silo. Slowly I turned and descended the silo step by step. One metal rail at a time, I got closer to the ground. Soon running around again in the yard as if nothing had happened.

Immediately I was told to "never do that again!" since it was about seventy-five feet high. Dad Saueressig gave me my first stern instructions. I did not know it at the time, but it almost scared the Saueressig family enough to not take us in as foster kids. They did anyway.

CHAPTER #5

Grammer School

With a huge garden, lots of animals, and a pet collie named Queenie, it was amazing what a wonderful place this was. They had a son named Russell in Illinois. He was starting his new job after graduating from college. When he came home for the weekend, he would wrestle with us even though we were little guys. He would take us both on at the same time. We were now his little brothers. We waited for his weekends home. Their other child was a daughter named Carol, who was still in high school. She was a kind and caring person and now our new older sister. Her boyfriend, Neal, came over to visit on many occasions. Somehow, he could not stay away long.

We would not get a visit from Karen for some time. When she came, we both were so excited to see her.

Mother and Father Saueressig started us in the local 4-H Club not long after arriving. As members, were told to be responsible and that each of us would have to take care of a calf on the farm. We were instructed to learn how to lead them around the yard, wash them, and feed them daily. Each of the calves got new names.

We also had other projects, like woodworking and cooking for boys in 4-H. It was hoped that we could take care of the calves well enough and win ribbons at the local Sheboygan County Fair. Winners would then be picked, and they would take them to the Wisconsin State Fair in Milwaukee. It was to compete with other clubs and kids throughout the state. We attended monthly meetings and participated in many activities that 4-H had to offer. We went on small trips, had cookouts, and went roller skating, along with many other forms of fun. It also provided us the opportunity to spend time with many other kids our age in our area.

———

It was a time when outdoor theaters or drive-ins were very popular. There were several in the area. Most larger towns had one. My new sister, Carol, took Dennis and me to our first experience at the drive-in theater. Carol and two of her girlfriends brought us to see the movie *Breakfast at Tiffany's*. I reminded her for years to come, with laughter, how we boys sure hated that movie. We were only nine and eleven years old by then.

"Couldn't we have gone to see a Godzilla movie or a Frankenstein movie?"

I now was in fourth grade and sent to an old one-room school out in the country. It was the last one-room school in Sheboygan County. It contained third, fourth, and fifth grades. It was called Scott Center School. It was just west of the little town of Batavia where we lived. A new school was being built in town, and we would attend that one the following year after they finished the construction. The new school would have grades one through eight.

This one was a very old school and had no plumbing at the time. There was a boy's bathroom in the back left side of the room, and the girls bathroom was in the back right side. These small rooms consisted of just enough room to move in and sit down on a wooden board with two large holes each. You would get in and out fast because of the bad smell alone.

This school was a larger building that had a big playground about two miles from our farmhouse in the country. Approximately thirty kids attended. The heating was provided by a coal-fire furnace in the basement. Someone was picked daily in class to shovel coal into the furnace when winter cold got to be too much. Even our little glass bottles of white or chocolate milk froze in the basement if we were not careful to cover them with an old blanket or use them up. On several occasions, I would drive my sister's old red bicycle to school if my new mother would allow me to in the spring or fall. I got teased a lot that first year but was happy to even have a girl's bicycle to ride.

Our new mom would pack us a small lunch in a paper bag for us to take to school. It always consisted of a sandwich, a big apple, maybe a pear, and a cupcake if we were lucky. Somehow carrot sticks found their way into the bag also.

Going to a new home was always awkward when calling her Mother or him Father. We were told to use whatever we were comfortable with at the time, so it took me usually longer than Dennis.

It did not take long for me to make a whole new set of friends at this school. Dennis was in sixth grade and at another school building in the middle of the little town of Batavia.

Trips to the local small lakes to go swimming became a regular thing for Dennis and a few of our friends. Usually the little lakes were only a mile or two away. We rode our bicycles and took a towel along .It was fun for each of us. It was an exciting time to spend together and with a few friends in the hot summer sun. We rode past farms and saw the country around us. We went exploring and stopping at the local A&W on occasion for a root beer or ice cream. We always had two of three of our friends with us.

It was also a time of discovery with the other kids. One kid thought it would be a great idea to show Dennis and me his new discovery at the beach. He called us over to the small building that was used as the changing room. It was a cement building with small booths and wooden plywood walls to change clothes. It had just four small stalls in there that you could put your trunks on. You could change back to your clothing when you were done swimming. All four stalls were in a row, and all the people went in one end and out another all day. The hot summer sun brought people here to swim and cool off. It was used by both girls and boys.

Our friend informed us that the wall between the girls and boys booths had several holes in it and we could see what the girls really looked like. Naturally, we all laughed at the opportunity, and soon we were all in one of the boys' booths together next to the girls. All five of us giggled as we pressed our faces to the wall that separated us from the girls. Peering into the holes in the thin plywood walls. There just happened to be four holes, and if there were more boys than holes, they would just have to wait their turn. No one inside, so we had to exit and watch for the next lady to enter the other side. We now lay close to the

entrance in the hot summer sun and the sand. We eagerly waited for someone to come and change. Soon we saw a lady, about
twenty-five to thirty, coming from the beach. She brought her
clothes along with her, ready to change and leave the beach. It
was time we whispered to each other.

The five of us rushed into the boys' changing stall. Each
small hole in the wall was taken, and the viewing was about to
start. Dennis was next to me, and we all started giggling, waiting
to see what would happen. I told them to keep quiet or she would
hear us, but it was almost impossible to keep them quiet in the
excitement. As she changed, we saw her nude body for the first
time. A hush came over us, and the giggling stopped. We now
saw something we all knew we would get in trouble for if we got
caught. Time seemed to stand still.

As the lady was about to put on her cloths, she leaned back
against the wall where each of us was peering through the holes.
She leaned enough to cover one of the boy's holes. He grumbled,
and we all laughed at his bad misfortune. We could see just fine.
He must have thought she would just move and give him a better view. So he poked his finger through the thin piece of wood
and poked right into her bottom. But just as he did it, she let out
a loud scream. She now knew what was happening. She turned
around. "Get out of here, you little brats! You are in big trouble!"
And out the door, we all stumbled over one another. Racing to
our bikes as if they were getaway cars.

We wished the bicycles could have been closer as we rushed
away to them. We hopped on them, and down the street we
went. Our little legs could not have pumped the pedals any faster. Down the road, we flew, one faster than the other. It was not
until we were far from the beach that we stopped and laughed

about our experience. We all agreed it was best not to go back to the beach for a long time. I asked the kid who did the poking, "Why did you do that?"

He had no answer, and it always brought out the laughing from us for years to come.

When we did return the following summer, the changing house was switched over to all brick walls between the boys' and girls' rooms. There would be no peeking anymore.

Dennis and I both got home from school at the same time even though he was at a different building for school. We rode the same bus home. I could spend a lot more time with him. It helped tremendously since I missed the rest of the real family so badly.

The farm was like a huge play area for Dennis and me. We would spend lots of time in the apple orchards, barn, and big front yard. We were lucky to have a large tractor tire swing that hung from a big tree in the front yard. We also spent lots of time at one or another of our new friends' in the country. One girl, about a ten-minute ride down the road, even had a monkey caged in their kitchen. We considered her fortunate to have a pet like we had never seen. We felt lucky also to each have an old used bicycle to ride that we'd found in a shed.

We were excited to each get a BB gun for Christmas that first year. Along with these, we received a new shirt and bow tie in a box. These were real presents we could each keep. We quickly pretended to hunt each other down on the big farm with our new rifles. There were so many places to hide.

Dennis and I agreed that we would not shoot each other if we were too close together. We also agreed that we must always shoot below the waist so we did not hurt each other. That idea did not last long for me for some reason.

Dennis and I would first hide from each other, and then the hunt for each other would begin. On one occasion, it took a long time for us to find each other. I could hear him at the end of the barn. I could not see him. I waited and waited for him to appear. Again, I could hear him but could not see him. The long wait got to me.

Finally, he poked his head around the corner. I decided I would wait for him to come out and then shoot his legs, but he never came all the way out. I would wait even more for him to peek out again. This time as soon as he showed his face, I would not hold back and let the shot go. Although I didn't know how powerful the BB guns were, my shot was accurate from fifty to seventy feet away. I could hear him yelp and squeal with pain. I knew I'd hit something on him. My BB pellet had found its mark.

I now rushed to his side to see how bad it was. I feared I had hit him in the eye, but fortunately I had hit him right between his eyes just above his nose. He was bent over on one knee with his hands on his face. A small trickle of blood moved slowly down one side of his nose. He could feel the little bullet or pellet just under the skin. He pleaded for me to help him get it out.

It was now time for me to help him, even though I was shaking hard. Together we pushed the BB around until we got it near the entrance hole. I then pinched it out at the hole. Dennis was really upset with me, but he told me not to say anything. We agreed that, if our new dad found out, we most likely would each loose our new BB guns.

Dennis later took my BB gun with him when he went to get the cows from the back field. He tossed it into the large water tank that the cows used on his way back to the house. I fished it out from the bottom of the tank the next day after he told me what he'd done. I knew I would never do something so stupid again as to shoot at him. Never did I want to make him feel bad again. My gun never worked properly after throwing it into the water tank, and I was ok with that because Dennis was good and he still loved his little brother.

Our new mom and dad were the best thing that could have happened to Dennis and me. Here was a family that was kind enough to take both of us in as foster kids, keeping us together and showing us a regular life. They were not only kind but good Christians who were willing to adopt us into their family and make us their own.

It was at this time that they came to us and asked us to sit in the living room so they could talk to us about something very import- ant. Dennis and I too wondered what would happen next. Would we be leaving for another home or maybe even back to the children's home again? To our surprise, the Saueressigs asked if they could adopt us. They did not tell us it was a done deal. They were asking us. We both were excited and confused about the kind act. What about our other real family? What did this all mean? Were we not wanted anymore by our real family? Surly they wanted us yet.

The Saueressigs explained it would be totally up to us, and we had time to decide.

Dennis and I talked it over for several days. Dennis was all for it, and I was not. I learned to love this family a lot. I really strug- gled with one point. Would I have to change my last name? Over and over, we talked about all the possibilities of being adopted. Dennis continually reminded me of the love these people had for us and how this was the best times of our young lives, especial- ly after the past ten years and all that went on in the children's home.

I explained to Dennis that I did not want to go through with it because I was born a Jackson and did not want to change my name. "We were born Jacksons, and we will always be Jacksons," I pleaded. "Not Saueressigs. What about our original family of Mom, Douglas, Ferris, Leo, and Karen? Do we just forget them? Will someone still come for us some day?"

Dennis soon relented, and we told the foster parents that we had decided to not get adopted. They said it was fine and that they would love us the same as their own kids, and they did.

They continually did that for years to come. By the time I was in high school, I understood I had better parents than most of my friends did. I got into a lot more mischief than Dennis, but I think it was my way of handling my frustrations being the youngest of the family that was broken.

It was one of these times, after being at this one-room school for a few months, that a girl in my class made me feel bad in front of the rest of the kids on the playground. She mocked me over and over about being a "foster kid" and not having "real" parents. She bullied me for some reason, and it finally got to me after several weeks. I now figured how I would fix her good.

Dale was a kid in my class, and we soon became good buddies. We played a lot together in the school yard. He was a little troublemaker like me, so we got along fine. As time passed, we would both get into trouble from something he was doing—or what I was up to.

It was on the playground that Dale would help me deal with Judy the girl who was giving me trouble. I decided that, while watching her laugh and have fun on the teeter-totter, I would get my revenge. I figured that it was the perfect time to pull off my best scheme yet. I searched out Dale to assist me.

I told Dale that, when she went down to the ground on her end of the teeter-totter, we would go to the other end and push that end down as hard as we could. I was sure we could launch Judy through the air. Yea, that surely would work, I thought. I was sure she would sail through the air high and far.

With excitement, we lay in wait like lions in the brush. Up and down they went, laughing, not knowing we were about to strike. Dale and I soon found the right moment. We rushed out from the bushes, both grabbing the high end of the teeter-totter. I was sure this girl was going to fly. We reached up and firmly grasped the end and pulled it down with all our weight. It was quick, and my plan was working fine.

That was until something happened I never planned on. She never let go of the teeter-totter handles! Oh, my goodness! She hung on tight to the handlebars with her hands as her feet and body went directly up in the air. I could see her feet straight up in the air against the bright blue sky.

She kept going over the top but never let go of her grip on the handles. Her body soon landed with a loud thump as she was now looking up in the sky. She was now completely on her back, lying on the board. It was now time for Dale and me to get away from there and hide as fast as possible. Other kids came rushing to help her when they heard the cries.

Several scooted inside to tell the teacher what had happened. There just were not enough places for us to hide. I could hear them clearly: "Bruce did it! Bruce did it!" It was inside and soon outside as the teacher arrived at the teeter-totter. I felt like running a long distance away but froze in one spot back in the bushes.

It wasn't long, and I felt the teacher's hand on my collar, pulling me inside. I don't think my shoes hit the ground once as she dragged me up the stairs and into the schoolroom. Dale and I were in big trouble this time, I thought.

Surprisingly, Dale never got blamed at all, and I never told her that he'd helped me.

Several weeks went by before I could go outside again and play. Plus, I got a seat right up close to the teacher's desk in the front row. She informed me she was going to watch me very closely from now on, and she did. I had to write on the chalk board a hundred times how sorry I was to Judy, and I would never do that again.

Judy was ok after that incident. Mostly scared more than anything. It was most likely the best thing she could have done to hang on until it was all over. She would pull a fast trick on me only a few years later when we went to the newly built grade school in Batavia.

It was Halloween, and we were instructed during the school day to come back at seven in the evening to go through the spook house that was built in the gym. It was an exciting time. The Spook House was all decorated by the local fire department with made up cardboard coffins, lots of passages with characters in masks, and lots of noises to scare us as we walked through it. It was a Spook House to remember. They did a great job as we all witnessed from those that went before us. We could hear the screaming and yells. Each group consisted of about six kids. The excitement was great, as our group of six were next to go in.

Judy, the girl I tried to launch through the air, sat directly behind me. All of us were jumping up and down with excitement. I did not know it, but this was her opportunity to get me back for the teeter-totter incident. Somehow, I never saw it coming. The teacher informed us that, if we did not quiet down and sit down, we were not going into the spook house next. We now rushed back to our seats. As soon as I sat down, I could feel the pain in my seat. I did not notice what she was up to. She got me good as she held a number-two pencil straight up with both hands. I had gone directly back to my seat and sat down quickly after the teacher's instructions. I was not about to miss getting into that Spook House. Immediately, I jumped straight up into the air, yelling, "Yeoooooowwww!"

This loud yell was not appreciated by the teacher, and she ordered me to the front of the class. "Get up here, Bruce!" she shouted. I held the pencil with one hand, since it was lodged in my seat, as I trotted up front to her. I tried to tell her quietly so all the other kids could not hear it, but she had me repeat it a second time even louder so she could hear.

"I got a pencil in my butt!" I exclaimed, and the whole room started laughing loud. She pulled me into the back room and had me turn around to inspect the damage.

It was well placed and firmly attached as she grabbed it and pulled it straight out. I was sure Judy had just got her revenge on me from when I tried to launch her through the air. She had planned it well, I thought. When I got home, I made no mention of the incident to my foster mom, but I felt I had learned another lesson. I would never forget that girl's name after that incident. It was Judy Ramminger. She had rammed me good all right. She moved away and went on to another high school that summer. I never saw her again after that year.

Attending the new school those years was a real joy. It had basketball courts where Dennis and I could spend hours playing one on one. It happened to be only a few blocks from our house in the little town of Batavia. Dad had sold his beautiful farm now after a few unfortunate farm accidents. The school also had a large baseball field, where we spent hours and hours playing baseball on teams we made up weekly.

Of course, with so many more kids on the school yard, some of the boys felt they had to show how tough they were. Who better to go after than those foster kids who didn't have real parents, as they said. One boy, who was a grade ahead of me in eighth grade, decided that I was his next victim. I knew who he was because I had heard he had pounded on several boys in the past. A big bully that many of the kids feared. Dennis was at the other school, and I could not depend on him to help me. I would have to handle this one alone.

The kid was easily five inches taller than me. It was my belief that he was bad only because he swore a lot. I never heard kids swear. Dad on the farm swore on occasion, but that was at the cows when he got angry with them. It was my belief that only adults swore, not kids.

This kid called me "Chicken Shit" because I told him I did not want to fight him. He then told the other kids gathering around us that "this little chicken shit doesn't know how to fight. I'm going to beat him up good tomorrow at recess. You all be there when I smack him around."

I went home with that kid on my mind all night. I lay awake most of the night. *What am I going to do?* I thought. He was so much taller, and he had those long arms. I was sure he could reach me easily. Worse yet, I knew he had two other brothers that were older than him. I was sure they would come after Dennis and me both. Would I go home tomorrow with large lumps on my head? How would I explain this to Dennis or to my new foster parents? Surely I did not want to get sent back to the children's home in Milwaukee.

The next day came way too soon. The recess bell rang, and the knot in my stomach felt as large as a watermelon. I entered the yard thinking that maybe that kid would have forgotten all about it. That idea was short lived when I heard him swearing and calling my name out. "Come on, Chicken Shit Bruce! Let's go! It's time."

Outside now, the group gathered around me with the tall kid directly across from me. He got closer and closer as I stared at those long dangling arms. I soon realized that the only chance I had in this fight was to get him closer to the ground so I could climb on top of him. Maybe closer to the ground, I had a chance. He made the first move, and I felt the breeze of his fist whiz by close to my face. I jumped back and realized that the next one would find its mark. Quickly now, I went down for his knees. I hung on tight as he tried to pound on my back. I kept the hold on him until he stumbled down to the ground. I could now see the surprise in his face from what was happening. We rolled over and over in the dirt.

I crawled on him more and more. I wanted to get closer to his face and start swinging. When the time was right, I let my right fist go, then the left. I could hear the yelling and screaming of the kids around us as I kept swinging at him over and over. Some even yelled my name, and it encouraged me even more.

I now found what I was looking for, and I started to hit his face again and again. My knees held his arms close on the ground. It must have been out of fear, but I swung over and over. I now saw the blood flow from his nose. I was sure he would leave me alone in the future if I pounded hard enough.

Then an unexpected feeling came over me as I triumphantly had this bully where I wanted him. The teacher pushed her way through the obvious group circle where we lay. She grabbed me by the collar, lifting me off him. Into school she sent us both to report to the principal's office.

The lady principle was aware of the bully and the many times he'd sat in front of her. She disciplined him and informed him that his parents would be contacted. Maybe even get expelled. I sat in fear that she would do the same for me, but it never happened. I just missed recess a few times and was told to behave myself out there.

Somehow the incident had a positive effect on me that year. Many kids talked about how I had beaten that bully. They even said I was the first person to take him down. Little did they know that fear would be with me for several weeks later. Would he come at me again? Or would he bring his brothers to find me at school or our house? We were lucky the bullies never bothered us again.

It was now 1963, and the reports of the Kennedys and the space program were on the news almost daily. We discussed the news stories in class as we were taught to be aware of what was happening around us. Time was quickly passing in our little town. It was one of these days that the teacher pulled the TV out from the back room. The tears flowed down her face as she set it up. She exclaimed something was happening and we should be aware of it because it was historic. We wondered what was happening as she turned on the black and white TV set in the front of the class.

Soon the news story told us how our president, John F. Kennedy, had just been shot in Dallas. A few hours later we were released from school. It was a very sad time, and even a few of the kids cried as we left school. As I returned home, the television was on in the living room, and Mother was also in tears. I was confused and did not know what to say or do. Never had we gone through something like this. I watched the set with confusion and sadness.

Only a day later, I saw the man who had been accused of killing our great president, Lee Harvey Oswald. I watched as he was paraded before the press and got shot by Jack Ruby right in front of the cameras. To my shock, it looked almost staged, and they would show it over and over. Somehow, I was glued to the TV the entire weekend. It was difficult to watch the funeral procession in the following days. The impression still stays with we me from when I saw the six black horses pulling the presidents casket down Pennsylvania Boulevard. We truly were witnessing history.

Later in life, I would visit Dallas on business and walk the same grounds and see where this all happened when I was young man. Walking on the grassy knoll and going up to the sixth floor of the book depository and finally crossing the street where it happened.

Mother Saueressig was a teacher for many years, and she insisted that we take schoolwork very serious too. When I wanted to go to the roller rink or spend time with my friends, she would always ask if the homework was done. She would ask if I knew my multiplication tables . If she quizzed me, and I slipped on one of them. I was told, "No going roller skating for you." She would get the cards out and practice with me for some time. I knew, if I did not learn them in a hurry, I would miss out on a lot of fun with my friends. Even playing baseball was a risk. I would now practice on my own. It did not take long.

CHAPTER #6

High School

High school came fast after a summer of fun in 1965. More and more, I would see cars that were slick and fast like Corvettes, Jaguars, Chevelle's, Pontiacs, and the new Mustangs. My interest grew more and more with each fall. It was fun anticipating the introduction of the new lineup of cars.

Dennis was in high school already, and his talk of a new girlfriend somehow made me laugh. I hoped I would have one someday too. Her name was Pam, and eventually they would marry when he returned from the navy. They were so much alike, and they seemed to be meant for each other because they always would be laughing together. Dennis did not have a car yet of his own. When he wanted to take her out, he would ask Dad for the use of the little yellow Volkswagen in the garage.

He once came home and had to explain to Dad that somehow the key had gotten broken out of the ignition while he was at the drive-in theater. Dennis tried to explain that he had turned the key too hard and it had just broken. Dad just laughed at his lame excuse and got it fixed the next day. No more was said. Dennis and I would laugh about this even several years later.

I did not attend any dances at the local firemen's hall until my sophomore year in high school. In our small town, it was a popular place for dances that were packed with kids every Friday night. If you did not attend Batavia Firemen's Hall on Friday, you sure had to be at Fillmore Hall on Saturday night; that was about twelve miles away. Each place brought in local bands and bands as far away as Milwaukee, Madison, and other states like Illinois or Minnesota. They were always packed and loud. Our little town had the best around, we thought.

When I was finally able to attend these dances, they were always exciting and fun. Most of my friends were there, and music got us dancing through every song. If you were not at the dances, you were at the drive-in theater with some friends or at a private party at someone's house or maybe a gravel pit. We paid one of our friends who had older brothers or cousins to get us some beer. It would be hidden in a ditch, and we were told where it was located so we could pick it up later. It worked great, and we always had beer or more available for our gatherings. Drinking age was eighteen for beer, and it was not hard to get someone to help us acquire our stuff at sixteen and seventeen while still in high school.

Drinking was quite common in the parking lots during these dances. If you were not drinking, you were getting intimately acquainted with someone .Sometimes there were a few hundred cars in the parking lot. I recall rows and rows of cars.

With so many kids at these dances, many came from different schools. The guys from our school were careful to stand in a half circle around the girls from our school. Most of the time, the boys were afraid to ask the girls to dance. It was like we were protecting them in our little half circle on the dance floor. Maybe four to six girls dancing and maybe five to ten of us watching close. We boys would discuss who we thought were the hottest ones. If you were scared to talk to them directly at school, maybe you might be brave enough to talk to them at the dance or maybe even ask them to dance.

On a few occasions, the girls even got into arguments with the girls from other schools. The boys usually brought it outside in the parking lot. It was our way to settle an argument with a fight or two. To my surprise, the girl I liked in school, who was a beautiful and quiet girl, got into a fight with another girl. The fight took place right in the middle of the dance floor. Words were exchanged, and soon the hair-pulling started. They next exchanged more than words. Soon the arms were flying about, and down to the floor they tumbled. Rolling now, over and over.

The boys yelled, "Go! Go!" in excitement. This was more exciting than the wrestlers we saw on television. The other girls soon pulled them both apart. It did not happen often, but occasionally we saw it. I was nervous to ask her to dance a slow dance when the time finally came, but this was my first opportunity to get close to her. My nerves were making me shake like a leaf. I could tell I was having a hard time speaking in her presence. The words just did not want to come out clearly. All I knew was her name was Carol and we were here at this special moment. Later we each went our own way, but we would attend the junior prom together in 1968. We would attend many class reunions for years and discuss these wonderful days.

I saw several fights in the parking lot of Batavia Fireman's Hall. One boy from our school stood out because he was just a sophomore but tough as can be. He often challenged the older kids in our school, but there were no takers. Even the senior boys stayed away from him. He feared no one. His name was Henry, and the dances always seemed to be an invite for him to find someone to fight. If not from our school , maybe another school.

He came to the dance one night and arrived with a kid that was a year older than him. That was because he was not old enough to drive or did not have a car. A kid from another school about twenty miles from ours got caught dancing with one of the girls from our school. Henry caught him on the dance floor and grabbed him. Henry punched him even though the kid was bigger than him. The kid from the other school made his second mistake by taking a few swings at Henry and telling him, "Let's take it outside."

Henry said, "Sure," and out to the parking lot they went.

Several of us followed them out to the gravel parking lot, and Henry got there first. There must have been ten to fifteen of us there to see what was going to happen. Henry had the keys to the car now and opened the trunk .I could only guess what he was going to get out for this encounter. In a short bit, he reached in, and out came the biggest chain in one hand and a tire iron in the other. I knew this was for real.

Fear must have overcome the kid from the other school in an instant, but he kept coming. Henry took a few swings with the chain, and it was over in a short time. The kid from the other school had blood streaming from his face when he walked away. His friends would help him back to his car.

Back to the dance we went; this was not fun to watch. The girls were much more fun to watch, and our time was going faster than we thought.

On another occasion at Batavia Hall, I recall standing in the circle watching the girls dance together because we were too shy to ask them to dance. We boys spoke to each other about how nice they looked when they danced—and so much better than in school. Before long, I got a tap on my shoulder.

I turned to look who it was, and to my surprise, it was my good friend Dale.

"Hey Bruce, you got to help me," he said.

I ignored his first plea and told him, "Dale, just watch the girls! They look just fine."

He tapped me on the shoulder a second time. "Hey. No. you really got to help me now!" "What do you want Dale? These girls look fine," I said.

He then explained what the problem was. He let me know the girl he had brought to this dance was in his car, and she was passed out cold. Somehow Dale thought I could save the situation. We slowly left the hall to go outside. I was curious to see what the problem was.

He proceeded to tell me how he'd picked up this very popular girl for a date. After they were at her house, they went parking and drinking at a different location before they got here. His explanation was that she'd been having fun drinking the booze and he'd just pretended that he was drinking it down, hardly swallowing a drop. He said he had hardly a few drops, and she drank it down like water, easily chugging it down.

We left the dance and slowly proceeded to the large parking lot. I did not see her at all until we got to the far side of the lot. As I got closer to inspect, I could now see her on the floor and partially on the front seat. She was out cold, with no clothes on.

"Dale! What did you do?" I shouted to him as he giggled like he always did. His explanation got stranger and stranger. He said that the more she drank, the more the clothes came off. He explained that he never drank much and only pretended when he lifted the bottle to his lips.

I asked him, "How come you have all your clothes on?"

He said, "I put it all on just to come in the dance to get you to help me."

"We have to get her back to her home, Dale," I said. "And now!"

Slowly we pulled her out from the car. We now could try and walk her around to sober her up and get her clothes back on. She kept falling to the ground and the grass in a big heap. We slowly tried to get her up and put on her undergarments on again and walk her around. She mumbled, and I could not make out a word of what she was saying. She would move a small distance at a time and fall again. She could only mumble a few words, and we had a hard time keeping her upright on her legs as we stood on each side, holding her. We stopped only to let her throw up. We walked more and more after I got her top and pants back on. Soon we had a bunch of boys standing around us. They were curious to see what we were doing. It was obvious to all who the popular girl was. They all imagined what we were up to, and it was not good.

Dale and I were getting very scared in our situation. We must have been out there in the parking lot for a half hour to forty-five minutes trying to assist her. I knew there were cops inside the dance hall. If we got caught out here, she would be in great trouble, and we would both be in a heap of trouble with her parents. I also knew that, if someone went back into the hall and told the cops, Dale and I could both end up at the cop shop. This would be a hard one to explain.

After working together, we were able to get her clothes all back on. Just the shoes yet, and it would be done. She lay on the back seat now, the shoes were easy to do. As we tried to get her out of the car, I heard someone in the crowd say, "I'll take my turn first."

All the guys started laughing and acting like a pack of wolves. I knew what they meant. I turned and exclaimed, "No one is going to touch this girl!" And soon we moved her back into the car. We slowly sat her in the front seat for the ride back to her house about ten miles to the east.

I told Dale, "Let's get the hell out of here before the cops get us." And we sped out of the lot with gravel flying and tires screaming.

We had about a ten-mile ride back to Random Lake, where her house was. It was in the city of Random Lake, and she lived close to the middle of town across from our football field. I knew right where we were going to get to her house. I heard her moaning, and I thought that was good because at least she was still alive. I informed Dale not to avoid parking directly in front of her house, but a few doors past.

When we arrived, we could see that the house was dark and no one was at home. It was quiet, and Dale stated that "her parents are going out for the evening, and if we can get her back in the house before they came back, we are free."

This was now a critical time because I was sure a neighbor would spot us. Maybe even the local cops would catch us trying to get her back into the house. How was I going to explain this jam? What would my foster parents have to say?

We slowly got her out of the car. She still had a hard time standing, but with our help under each arm, she slowly stood up and started to take small steps as we turned to the house. We all carefully moved closer and closer to the house. The door was not locked, and we slowly crept inside looking for the stairway to her room.

After questioning her, I learned through her slurring, her room was upstairs to the right. I was hoping it was on the main floor, but we had to get her up the stairs and get out of here as soon as we could.

Step by step we went up the stairs. We both agreed that, when we got to her room, it was not a good idea to put her pajamas on. We would tuck her under the covers with her clothes all on and get out of here. She could explain why she was dressed to her mother in the morning if she had to.

We now moved toward the door, and a noise came from downstairs. The side door was opening from the garage. Her mother and father were now getting home and coming inside. They chatted as they came into the house. We instantly froze and crouched down by the side of our friend's bed. I heard her father and mother talking downstairs. They then proceeded to their bedroom. All Dale and I could do was wait until it was quiet after they went to bed. Dale started laughing, and I begged him to be quiet. After a while of listening to the bed squeaking downstairs, I feared her mother or father would come up stairs and catch us.

About hour or more passed, and finally it got quiet downstairs. I heard no voices or bed squeaks. Dale wanted to go back downstairs to leave, and I said "No way! We sure are going to get caught by her father. What if he has a gun?"

I looked around to see what we could do next. I soon realized that the window was our only way out of here. I now opened the window very carefully.

The tree in the yard was between the house and the garage. It was large enough and close enough for us to climb from the house to a limb on the tree. The large branches were big enough to handle both of us as we slowly moved closer to the ground. Down we went branch by branch.

The car was parked only a short distance away, and we were relieved to reach it in a hurry. Somehow, we now knew we could get away. We slowly drove out of town, straining to see if the cops were following us. It was not until we got to the outskirts of town, that we lit up a cigarette with the joy of escaping. We never spoke of this evening again.

It was like we had just escaped Alcatraz prison.

Back to the teen lounge we went. It was an old brewery converted into a teen lounge hang out with a small restaurant that served hotdogs, hamburgers, fries, and malts, as well as a juke box that played all our favorite music. It was a fun place of choice and a where we could get together. There were only a few places to escape for our young crowd.

When school resumed on Monday, I avoided her and Dale for a long time. I did not want to be associated with what had happened. I had hoped she would not remember a bit of it, and I knew Dale did too. I knew she had to wonder that following morning, how she'd gotten back home and back into her bed. I now was hoping she would not point any fingers at Dale or me.

The school parties among us in the different groups at a school continued throughout the year. The different groups in our small school consisted of what we called brainiacs, jocks, party kids, farm kids, and others. You could be part of several groups if you liked. With only slightly over four hundred kids in the high school, you knew everyone and what classification they fit into. You knew their names, where they lived, and who they hung around with.

It was the night before homecoming now in 1968, and it had been a tradition for years to decorate the gym the night before the dance. It usually reflected the theme of the night. This year's theme was Camelot, and our committee would go all out to fill the gym with streamers, large wording on the walls, a drawbridge with a castle image, and even a punch stand on one side.

I oversaw the punch stand. I would put together a nice little stand with the help of a few of my buddies on the decorating committee. We pounded it together and brought the pieces into the gym to assemble. When finished, it turned out great with a fake grassy roof and more. Room for a few servers of punch with snacks like popcorn and chips.

Of course, it was also a tradition to have a big party with those on the committee and others after all the decorating was finished. A place for this ordeal was picked out at someone's gravel pit, and we were set to go. We each decided what we would bring to party. A bottle of booze or two, beer, wine, some soda, or snacks to the predesignated location. Usually it would be in a gravel pit, but sometime at someone's house if maybe the parents were gone.

The preparations started a few days before the big night of decorating. The excitement was overwhelming, and the word soon was out. Everyone knew that the party would be happening as soon as the decorating was done Friday night after the big football game. We knew to keep it quiet so no parents would catch on. The decorating went great as all the parts in the gym came together. Everyone looked forward to the decorating party after decorating the gym was done. The big dance would be Saturday the next night.

I was so excited for the upcoming days and had asked a little blond girl to go with me. Her name was Sandy. She was in the gym decorating along with the rest of us. We both were so excited to be going to the dance. The committee consisted of about fifteen to do the complete job, and it turned out fantastic. We were proud and could hardly contain our excitement as we finished the gym. Some of the teachers were there too. Several teachers commented that this was the finest homecoming decorations they had ever seen.

We soon jumped into several cars to proceed to the party. The group grew to about thirty kids as word quickly got out to the others. A lot more liquor arrived than we planned, and a large variety of booze like I had never seen. We even put together what was called a "Whop-a-Tully." It consisted of a large bowl or tub where we poured every different type of booze and wine we brought together. Beer was separately put in a cooler with ice. We then would dip our paper cups into the Whop-a-tully tub and fill them up to drink the alcohol concoction we made up at the time.

Sometimes some soda was added if it got too strong, but mostly the booze and cheap wine were mixed. After filling the bowls a few times, everyone got louder and the fun progressed.

The music blasted, and we now had our big party well on its way. The music was just loud enough that we had to yell to talk to one another. We now strained to speak to one another over the music, but we were a happy bunch. We talked about the big day tomorrow and who we were going with to the dance. We also discussed those picked for the homecoming court. The excitement was overwhelming as we drank more and more. The time passed quickly, and the party got louder and louder as more kids attended than we expected. More bottles got poured into the large bowls, and more beer arrived. It was a happy time that we thought would never end in our young lives.

I knew I was supposed to arrive home by 1:00 a.m., a little longer than usual. I requested it because I had informed Mother and Father Saueressig that I was on the committee to get the gym decorated for homecoming. They soon agreed about the time to be home.

They were firm foster parents and I knew a few minutes either way would be tolerated, but not much.

One o'clock came and went, and the booze was taking effect. We hooped and hollered and sang along with the music. I thought everything would be fine if I just got into our house and went to bed. What could go wrong? I thought I had it made. Tomorrow was going to be so much fun.

After I'd stumbled a few times, my friends thought it might be a good idea for me to get home. We always watched out for each other because we were such a close group. They knew my parents were strict and might not be happy if I was late.

Out to the cars we went. With their assistance, I was put into my friend's car, and we headed home. Home was only about fifteen miles away. Even that seem like a long way. I knew a stop was necessary halfway there. It was not only to relieve myself, but my last meal of snacks were about to come up again. We all knew that throwing up was ok. if we got out of the car in time. I knew it had to be quick because it was now 2:30 a.m.

I seemed to reason that Mom and Dad would be sound asleep by the time I arrived to sneak into the house. They always went to bed early.

I was dropped off in front of our house, and I staggered across the grass and close to the front door. I'd sat at the front door on the steps for what must have been several minutes when I heard my friends yelling, "Go inside! Go inside!" Slowly I stood up and turned carefully toward the door.

I slowly opened it and entered our house. Trying to be as quiet as I could, I removed my shoes so I could silently move down the hall. Somehow, I believed I could do this, no matter how difficult. My room was not too far now. "Why is it so extremely hot in here?" I asked myself.

Mother and Father's room happened to be directly across from Dennis's and mine at the end of the hallway. Quietly, I now I slid down the hall in my socks, thinking how hot it was in the house compared to the cool air outside. The sweat was now starting to run down on my face. Maybe out of fear or because I still had my big letterman's jacket on, it seemed to get hotter and hotter. There were no obstacles in my way. It was a straight shot to my room. It was only twenty feet down the hall. I noticed all the pictures on the wall as I slowly started sliding along the wall that was now holding me up.

Only a few more feet, and I was home free to my bedroom when I heard a voice. It was Mother. "Bruce!" Her door was cracked open only a few inches with her light on the headboard. She asked me, "How did it go?" as I strained to hear her. I replied as best as I could.

"It went fine. The punch stand has grass on the roof."

She then asked again, a bit louder, "What else do they have?"

I could see her reading light on. I couldn't think of anything else to say, and I repeated, "The grass is on the punch stand."

Now, she knew something was wrong, and Dad did too as I repeated the same words the second time, praying the wall would not give in.

He sat up in bed and turned on his reading light above their heads. He said with authority, loud and clear, "Bruce! she asked you what else do they have."

Now the heat was unbearable, and my brain could not make sense of what was happening. My heart seemed to beat faster and faster. All I could think of came out in a louder slurred voice. "The punch stand has grass on top!" Now, I could no longer hear their voices, and everything went blank. The darkness now overcame me. I could no longer use my legs, and down I went hitting the floor with a bang.

As I fell forward, my head slammed on their bedroom door. The door then banged hard against the inside wall of their room and returned a second time to hit me hard again on the forehead. I finally made it to the floor inside their bedroom.

Now Dad jumped out of his bed in a flash. Mother exclaimed, "He must have been drinking!"

The next thing I felt was Dad grabbing me with both hands to pull me off the floor. "You little bastard!" he yelled as he called for Dennis to help him.

Dennis was soon at his side, and they dragged me over to my bed across the hall. Into the bed, I got dumped, and Dennis put the covers over me. I heard Dad say, "I'll deal with him in the morning!"

It was only a few seconds as they all stood at my bedside. I could feel the room start to spin around and around me. This was not good. I knew it, and I finally shouted, "Make it stop!"

Jumping up to try and make it stop spinning, I knew I was going to throw up. Everything wanted out. I pushed Dennis and Dad apart in my attempt to reach the bathroom in time, but with no luck. The bathroom was not close enough, and I soon everything came up in the hallway. Now swearing started again. I could hear Dad say lots more as he told me to clean this mess up with Dennis.

The morning came quickly, and Dennis was still in his bed next to mine when I woke up. I was still feeling very rotten as I moved around. Dennis was giggling at the situation I was in.

He said "Boy, are you in big trouble. Dad is very angry with you, and you are going to get it."

His gloating advice did not help me feel any better as I slowly moved about and got out of bed. The head ached, and it was pounding inside me. I felt the bruises from when I fell and hit the floor. The large bump on my head was my proof that not all was good from last night.

After I took a shower, I heard Dad and Mother at the kitchen table calling me from our bedroom. Dennis looked at me with a big smile from ear to ear. He relished the moment, and I knew all hell was coming my way. I went to the kitchen table and sat down. I could see they were both very upset with me. They must have discussed what my punishment was going to be before I arrived. Dad immediately asked if I had a date for the homecoming dance tonight.

I replied, "Yes. With Sandy."

He grabbed the phone on the table and banged it down hard in front of me. "No, you don't! You call her right now and tell her you are not going! I don't care how you tell her, but you are grounded for several weeks."

I stared at the phone sitting at the table in front of me now. How was I going to make that call? What would I say to her? I waited several hours to get up the nerve to call her. Mother encouraged me to hurry up so she could make other plans.

Nervous now, I could hear the ringing of Sandy's phone. Her mother answered, and I politely asked for Sandy. She came to the phone, and I quickly apologized to her that I could not take her to the dance. I explained I was grounded for several weeks and I would be at home. To my surprise, she said that was ok; she understood, since she was at the party also. She was in the car also when they dropped me off. She had encouraged me to get inside. She explained she'd seen me at the party and helped with several others. She wondered what would happen with my strict parents if I got caught. She was very understanding.

The hours passed, and I tried to stay out of sight. I thought if I stayed in my room, I would not get Dad and Mother any more upset. I knew I had disappointed them. I knew all my friends were going to have a great time as the time drew near for the dance. It was now seven p.m., and the front doorbell rang. Mother went to answer it. A few words were exchanged, and Mother called me over to the front door. To my shock, it was Sandy with a few of our friends from the night before.

Sandy said that they were on their way to the dance and thought they would stop by. Slowly she presented a small flower from behind her back. It was supposed to be on my suite for the dance, she told me. She pinned it on my shirt, and I felt lower than I ever could have. This is not what I wanted to happen. This was the worst punishment I could have gotten from my parents, but I knew it was my fault alone. Never again would I be getting home late or drunk, I did not want disappoint them like this again.

By the time I was a junior in high school, I started to tell Mother and Father I wanted a car. I spent more time with Mother since Dad now worked in the foundry at Kohler Company a lot of hours. The big farm was sold, and we moved into the small town of Batavia. Dad would build a new house close to our church.

She mentioned it to him when I was home on a Saturday. She suggested maybe Dad and I could go and look at some cars today. Maybe at the little Studebaker dealer not too far away. Dad agreed to only purchase a car if I would pay for half of it. I had saved up for several summers of working on farms and mowing lawns in the area and that sounded fine to me. The excitement was almost overwhelming.

As we arrived at the dealership, I knew Dad was familiar with the owner after they had a hearty greeting. His name was Ray, and he had one of the last Studebaker dealerships still open in the state. He proceeded to show us several old Studebakers and some other ugly cars in the small lot. I hated those boxy cars from the late fifties and early sixties. Ray soon realized I did not like any of the cars he had on his small lot of twenty cars. I did not know it at the time, but I was getting spoiled from such a great life.

"I don't think he likes any of these, Ervin," Ray said.

I told my dad, "I would never drive one of these Studebakers to school because my friends would laugh me out of school." Ray replied that he did have a few more cars in a large shed in town and maybe we would like to check them out before we left.

"Maybe there is something in there he will like."

We drove only about eight blocks away and stopped at a large metal building. Ray hopped out of his car and slid the doors of the large shed to the sides, and there it was. It seemed to jump out at me with all its beauty, and I was sure we did not have to look any further. I wanted it as soon as I saw it. It was a 1964 Chevrolet Chevelle convertible. It was dark blue with a black soft top and a light blue interior. It was only a few years old. It was in beautiful condition with low mileage. I told Dad, "This is it."

He asked me if I had half the twelve hundred dollars the dealer wanted for the car. I eagerly said, "I sure do," and the car was purchased. Somehow, I felt this car was waiting just for me. Dad and I were told to pick it up a few days later, after they called and got it shined up and ready for me.

The day arrived for Dad and me to pick up the car. I nervously hopped into Dad's Volkswagen and could hardly talk as Dad gave me the pep talk about driving safely with this new car of mine. All I could think of was taking the girls to the drive-in theaters and going to the dances all over.

I polished that car over and over. I was so proud to show it off.

Of course, I pleaded to take it to school as soon as they would let me. It was a carefree time, and I hoped it would never end.

Since I did not have a huge engine like some of my friends, I never raced it but one time. It looked as sharp as could be, and the girls loved it with the top down.

Our senior year brought three exchange students to our school. One was a beautiful short girl with long black hair down her back. It was the longest I had ever seen on a girl. Her name was Marta.

She attended a dance at school and saw the Chevelle I was showing off to my friends. She asked if it was my car. "Of course," I said and offered her a ride. We took off down the road, Marta sitting close to my side. Down the street we went as I pushed up the speed to impress her. She giggled with excitement. The further we went down the road, the more difficult it became for me to drive. Her long, long, black hair blew up and into my face as I pushed it aside over and over again. I decided it was going to be a short ride. I wanted to get back right away and keep her safe.

———

She hopped out and thanked me over and over. Throughout the year, as she spent the year at school, she reminded me of the nice ride she had in that beautiful convertible.

We were fortunate to have three foreign exchange students as the fall and last year of high school neared.

One of the other students came from Finland; he was a thin blond-haired boy that wanted to belong to the fun drinking group in our class. He happened to ask me one day, "Do they drink beer here in Wisconsin?" Several of the kids we were with started laughing.

"Why, of course they do," I said. "We are famous for beer. We have lots of breweries here, and they make lots of beer."

His name was Valto, and he was ready to attend one of our parties. He was highly intelligent and just wanted to fit in with us and have fun while he was at Random Lake High in our final year.

I brought him to several parties, and he asked me on several occasions, "Where is the next party?"

I knew I had to be careful and discreet with Valto because his US parents and my parents went to the same church in our little town of Batavia.

It was a period of eighteen-year-old drinking bars before twenty-one age limits started. They were scattered throughout the state. Since we were too young to gain entrance, fake identifications were the only way to get into the bars or we had to wait until after we graduated and turned eighteen.

They were very popular since they had great bands and loads of people from long distances. The big city of Milwaukee had a twenty-one age limit, so lots of younger kids from Milwaukee traveled forty miles to get into the clubs near us.

Valto inquired about these places, and I informed him that there was one such club just north of Port Washington, Wisconsin. It was a bit too close to us, and I determined it would be too easy to be caught—or our parents would find out.

I told him about another such club near Sheboygan, Wisconsin, that had great bands every weekend. It was called Club 23.

He was determined to go to Sheboygan's Club 23 and get into the place to see what it was like. He told me, "We need to go this place next weekend."

I was nervous now because I knew he did not have a car. I felt I should take him next weekend so he got home safe. If he was drinking, we could go and only stay a short time. We could get back home at a good time.

The following Saturday came, and it was time to make the trip to Sheboygan's Club 23.

The place was packed when we arrived, and we could hear the music out in the far side of the parking lot before we stepped to the entrance. I could see Valto was so excited to get into the place. We got in without any problems, and Valto and I celebrated with cans of Pabst Beer to start. They started to flow and go down with ease. Before we knew it, the band was playing their last song for the night. I knew I had about thirty miles to get back home.

The trip was slowly covered as I carefully drove back to our teen lounge. We would eat something before going home. I jumped out and we both agreed that a burger, fries and Coke would be great before the trip back to the Batavia area.

I jumped out of the car, and in I went. I said hi to a few friends on my way in, and they asked me where Valto was.

I said, "He is coming in right away."

Soon, I missed Valto and went back out to my car to find him. He was not there. I was scared now and asked some friends to help me find him.

After about twenty minutes of looking in the parking lot and the grassy field next to it, I looked in each of the ten cars that were there. "Here he is!" someone yelled.

He had crawled into a car that was parked on the street and not in the parking. A total strangers car.

I got him home safely, but his parents here did not find out about our trip to the club. We were just home late. They called my parents because we were a little late, but not much happened after that. They reminded Valto to behave or he would be returning to Finland before he graduated in '69. After that, we did not see Valto and any of the parties.

CHAPTER #7

Summer Job

Dennis went into the Navy, and I spent my final year in high school alone. Several more parties and several more dances at the firemen's hall or at school were coming to an end. It was now time to decide what I would be doing for the summer.

My three other closest friends had decided what they were going to do. Going into college or into business. We'd called ourselves the "Fearsome Foursome" for the past four years because of the double dating, going to the drive-in theaters, dances, and parties. We were the best of friends. When we were not going out, we got together playing poker and drinking beer. They were truly the best of friends, and it was the best of times.

Before school was over, Mother and Father Saueressig reminded me that it was time for me to decide what I was going to do when high school was over. The summer was coming on fast.

"You are not going to one of the big colleges like Madison or Oshkosh University," they exclaimed. "Because all they do is party, drink, and smoke pot! You should attend a technical college to learn a trade, like your cousin."

My foster cousin was a barber in a small town only about ten miles from our house.

The more I thought about it, the better it sounded to me. I knew Green Bay had a technical college that taught barbering, and if I could get accepted, it had to be better than this tiny town of Batavia with only ninety people. My parents apparently did not know how large Green Bay was and that they partied there like any other town.

I applied for barber school, and after several weeks, I received an acceptance letter in the mail to attend Northeast Wisconsin Technical College in Green Bay.

Mother and Father were so excited too. They would tell all the relatives and neighbors with pride. I couldn't help but feel they would be relieved when I left after all the trouble I gave them the previous four years. I knew I still had to get a job over the summer to get some money.

It was at a time when lots of companies were hiring. The newspaper was filled with want ads and pages of companies looking for help. Dad had worked at Kohler Company now, and I thought that it would be a good place for me to work also over the summer before college.

I went over to the employment office right after my graduation. Only a few days later, I got a call to come to work the following Monday. Excited to work and get some money before I went to technical college in the fall, I knew it could not have worked out better.

Dave and I both had midsized cars. He had a Mercury Cyclone, and I had that Chevrolet Chevelle Convertible. When we met at the designated spot, we pulled up close to each other, side by side. He asked if I wanted to race him to the next intersection, which was another mile down the road, since we were in the country.

I reluctantly agreed, and we were soon going down the road. He was ahead of me for a while, and I soon caught him. Together we floated down the road with no one heading our way from the opposite direction. I was now ahead of him with Dave now catching up. We looked at each other and smiled. We pressed it even harder now as our engines thrust us forward. I looked down, and my needle now was at ninety miles an hour. I recalled it was a beautifully warm day, and the sun was bright that afternoon.

I had my car filled with gas and oil at the garage earlier and knew I had plenty of gas. I did not realize what was about to happen. The hood shook a bit, and before I knew it, it had flown straight up into the air in front of me, blocking my entire view. Flying up so hard, it bent over the top edge of the windshield. I could not see any road in front of me. Thankfully, my side window was open wide, and I quickly put my head out the side to see where I was going.

I was shaking hard as I got into my car to stop on the side of the road. All I could see now was Dave flying down the road, getting farther and farther away from me. I hopped out of the car and pulled the bent-up hood back down to position as best as I could. I fortunately found a wire hanger in the trunk and secured the hood back down. It looked bad, but I now figured how it had happened. The garage worker where I had the fill up with gas and check the oil had never put the hood down far enough or latch it tight. I never noticed either when I left to meet Dave.

We both met the girls, and I was embarrassed at how my beautiful car now looked. Someone even asked if an elephant had fallen on my car. That brought several laughs. It took a while before I got it to the body shop and even longer to get it fixed. It was shortly before I went on to Green Bay and college.

I was involved in several sports in school. I was on the first wrestling team that started my freshman year. Football was my favorite, and I made the varsity team the first year as a freshman. I and one other guy named Tom Goetch were the only freshman selected. He would proudly remind me at each class reunion through the years. He was a likeable guy who was very popular in school also.

Graduation in early June came, and the evening program brought a few surprises. Dad and Mom came with a few others to see my graduation. It made me feel like I had a real family.

I was asked to sit near the front with all those that were going to receive scholarships. I wondered why they would want me to sit up there.

As they read off the names of all the different scholarships, each person proceeded to the front, and the crowd clapped respectfully.

The scholarship for technical school was next, and I totally did not expect it. They announced my name, and I nervously went up to get it. They shook my hand, and I looked out to the crowd to see my foster parents. I got to share a very great moment everyone afterward.

I now had to be sure to have a job for the summer before college. Kohler Company seemed like a good choice since father Saueressig was working there already. I applied the following Monday.

CHAPTER # 8

Off To Green Bay

A week and a half passed, and the next Saturday came to make my trip to Green Bay. It was a bright day. The temperature was already rising in the morning to seventy degrees. I was up early since I knew it would take a few hours to get there from where we lived. Mother was always up early with breakfast in the air. She reminded me to "eat something before I left on my long trip. You do not want to get hungry before you get home."

I had filled my car with gas and oil the night before, so I was ready for the long trip.

I knew I would be driving my convertible, and I was excited about it. It would be my longest drive since I purchased the car a year or so ago.

I wore a pair of shorts and a short sleeve shirt. I wanted to get going and get back so I could go out on a date later that night. I jumped into the car and started it up. I slowly put the top down on the Chevelle. It was going to be a hot day, and I was ready for it.

To my surprise, Mother jumped into the front seat next to me. She wore a pair of pants with nice blouse. She also wore a larger scarf around her little face, along with a little pair of sun-glasses. She was small sitting next to me and most likely not over a hundred pounds.

Being a bit embarrassed, I asked her "What is going on?"

She replied like a Mother would: "You didn't think you were going to find a place on your own, did you? I'm going with you. Dad and I want to make sure you get a decent, clean place to live. No party house for you! Let's go."

I slowly drove the convertible out of the little town of Batavia and headed toward Green Bay. The drive was fun, even if it was with my mother. I think she liked it too. It was the best quality time I had never spent with her, and it gave us time to talk like we never did earlier.

The hot wind blew as we cruised down the highway. She re-minded me on several occasions to "slow down and check the speed limit." Just like a mom would.

We arrived at Green Bay an hour and a half later. We drove around to check where the school was and if there were any apartments close to school. After several stops, we soon learned that we should have gotten here sooner to find a place. Lots of students were here already.

At one location, a gas-station and food-store lady reminded us to check on the bulletin board at the college. She claimed that several apartments may be looking for tenants and several people even rented out rooms to students in town. Mom thought that it was a good place to check, and I agreed. We headed over to the college to find that bulletin board.

We hurried, since we agreed that it was a good idea and we did not want to waste time. We got inside of school and found the big bulletin board. It was full of small notes and cards of people looking to rent out a room or looking for a partner to share an apartment—and lots more.

One note caught my attention, and I shared it with mother after I read it over.

It read, "Room for rent. For men only!"

And it had a phone number and a street location in town.

As we looked it over, we realized that it was not too far from where we were located. We were on Broadway Ave. The rental spot was about twelve blocks away to the north on 711 North Ashland Ave.

Back into the car, we went, and we were soon searching for the location. We had a Green Bay map, and Mother directed me to the spot since we were never in town before.

It was a large two-story white house in the middle of the block. The smell of the large paper companies in Green Bay permeated the air throughout the town. Mother complained about it several times, but I did not mind it. I later found that it was common if the wind was in the right direction from east to west where we were.

We walked up to the front door, and I nervously rang the doorbell. To my surprise, a small, round little lady, about five feet high, with pure white hair, answered the door. We asked her, "Is this the place that rents to men only?"

She looked us up and down, checking us closely. I thought it funny as she looked at Mom to.

Before she would answer, she pointed her finger at me and asked, "Do you smoke?"

I was taken aback by the question as I looked over at Mother. I knew I smoked, and Mother knew it too. I did not want to lie in front of Mother. I said, "Yes," in dismay.

I then started to turn to go back to the car. Mother was close behind me when the little whitehaired lady said she would show us the room for rent anyway: "C'mon in if you like."

We turned back toward her out of courtesy and slowly entered the big house.

She brought us upstairs and walked us around. She pointed to a bathroom and said it was one I would use. I saw several guys in the house, but most were older. She proudly would show each of the bedrooms available and the kitchen that we could use between certain hours. She was proud of the room she claimed would be possibly mine with the bathroom near and the nice porch. It also had a small study room in the rear. A larger bed with a big bedspread filled most of the room. As we proceeded downstairs and stood in the living room, she said, "Joe sits there. Mike sits there. Harold sits over there. And this big chair here could be yours."

I knew we had to get going if we were going to find a room. I knew she had already asked about the smoking. I had to find something, as it was getting later now. We also had a long drive to get back home.

"Maybe we could return next week," Mother said. Mother and I moved slowly toward the door. As we got back on the front porch, the lady was close behind us. She then pointed her finger straight at me again and asked, "Do you smoke?"

I said, "Come on, Mom. Let's go find a room."

The lady then said, "You can only have the room if you smoke! I don't rent to people who don't smoke!"

Mother and I stared at each other in surprise. How could this be? The lady rented rooms to guys who only smoked? No nonsmokers allowed. How fantastic and lucky I felt. This was perfect since it was only about twelve blocks from the school. We turned and told the little woman that we would be glad to rent the room.

I stayed at the house there on North Ashland for a full year. I quickly got two jobs to pay the rent and to party on many occasions. One being a janitor after school and one being a busboy at a restaurant called the Blackstone. It was a very popular family restaurant. The two heavy-set ladies that owned the restaurant always made sure I had enough to eat.

The little white-haired lady that owned the house and rented rooms explained the rules of the house and why she rented to smokers only. Her reason was that she'd been informed by her doctor that she would have to quit smoking immediately and have a lung operation if she wanted to live. She had smoked for many years, and she had reached a critical point in her life.

The doctor said that, if she quit, she could possibly live several years after her lung operation. She exclaimed to me that, after she'd had heard that, she quit immediately. She also said she promised the Lord she would never pick up another cigarette if she got through the lung operation ok.

I learned after only a few days later that one other person smoked cigarettes, two smoked cigars, one smoked a pipe—and then there was me.

I got home from school at about 4:00 p.m. daily. She would be sitting in the living room waiting for me if no one else was home. She nervously moved about back and forth until I lit up my cigarette. If I was slow at it, she reminded me to "hurry up and light that thing up. What's taking so long?" It always had the soothing affect she was looking for.

One of my roommates was a young teacher in town only a few years older than me. He also was the goalie for the Green

Bay Bobcats hockey team. His name was Mike, and he was hoping to be selected to play for a big professional team in the next draft. It was fun to be around him because he was very popular in town. The ladies just loved him and often asked me if I played hockey also. I just went along with it, not to disappoint them.

He broke the number one rule in the house on many occasions: "No women in the house." If I came home late from being out or was awakened in the middle of the night, I could hear him trying to sneak up the stairs with a beautiful date. The squeaky steps were a sure give-away, but the little old lady never heard a thing. They would have their backs close to the wall as they came up. We would bump into each other doing this every once and a while. The landlord lady was a heavy sleeper, and neither of us ever got caught.

CHAPTER #9

The Apprenticeship

After my year of school, my apprenticeship would be in Appleton, Wisconsin on the main street called College Avenue. It was the fall of 1970, and I now drove a big white 1964 Chevrolet Impala. I was the highest-paid apprentice from my graduating class. I got paid sixty dollars cash a week, and I thought I was rich.

Finding a place to live did not take long after sleeping in my car a few days. Someone in the shop had suggested a place off College Ave. on Drew Street, about eight blocks from the shop. They called it Independence House because there were eight guys that lived there, going to the college or working close. I found the place great since it was only blocks from our barber shop, where I worked and there was all the downtown activity. I could arrive to work in only a few minutes even if I walked. It was called The Uptown Barber Shop.

I arrived to find a big two-story house. It held several guys and a young gent who managed it. The house had five large bedrooms, and several were big enough for two or three people and beds. The man that managed it was about twenty-five years old.

He took some courses at Lawrence University only six blocks away from the house.

He had me fill out a piece of paper and told me the rules of the house were very simple. He explained there were only a few rules. 1) Pay your rent on time. 2) No fighting. And 3) there must always be beer and doughnuts in the refrigerator. That sounded good to me. Also, the small amount of rent of only forty dollars a month convinced me that this place could work well for me. After a while, I made several trips with my new friends to pick up the day-old donuts at several locations in Appleton. We quickly knew what places would give us those donuts on our weekly trek.

They would give them to us free. We always said it was "a house for down-and-out men. Down on their luck. And a place they could stay and not be on the sidewalk." That plea always worked well on the donut shop managers. I recall several places that were pleased to give us several dozen donuts. It was not un-usual to have many dozen donuts on hand and cases of beer. We called it Independent House. It was truly an exciting place and a growing experience.

Since we were withiin walking distance to several bars and clubs, it was always fun in this college town. College Avenue or the main street through town was busy with pizza shops, bars, banks, and lots of shopping. It was one of these times I leaned to be careful who to hang out with.

After a few weeks, I learned where the hot spots were and where most of the college kids hung out.

It was about 9:00 p.m. on a Friday night when I informed my good friend Tom that I would be going downtown to several of the busy college bars. I dumped on the cologne and imagined the girls could not resist me if I got close. Tom agreed to go along.

He was a shorter guy who was stocky and very friendly. Another guy named Bob lay on the couch near us. Bob was a tall guy, well over six feet. He was a very slow young man that had trouble speaking clearly. He was on assistance while he stayed here and never worked a day while I knew him. He never washed much, and his odor was gross. His own family had thrown him out several years earlier.

Bob jumped up as soon as he heard me discuss my plans for the evening. "I want to go too," Bob mumbled. "I want to go with you guys."

I knew this was going to be a situation I had to resolve right away. "No, Bob, we are going to find the ladies tonight, and we can only do this with just the two of us."

Bob did not like that answer, and he pleaded with us again to take him along with. "Come on, you guys. Take me too."

The guy who managed the house sided with Bob. He suggested we take Bob with us because it would be good that Bob get out for a while—then he would be no problem. I shuttered to think how lucky we could be connecting with any of the girls if Bob was straggling along.

I soon relented and told him he could go with us. I told him he had to move away from us if we were talking to one of the beautiful ladies. I also instructed him to keep his mouth shut if we were talking to any girls: "If you see us starting to score, you must walk away!" He agreed, and we started to walk downtown. It was not far, only a block to the main street. And I was excited to go.

The first place a few blocks away was called The Music Box. It was a lower-basement club and crowded from one end to the other. I tried to move away from smelly Bob as soon as we got in. It was difficult because he only knew us and wanted to stay close to us. It seemed that every time I turned around, Bob was standing right there. He towered above the crowd. The music had everyone in a great mood. The crowd was lively, and the place was packed, which made it difficult to move from one end to the other.

After a few beers, Tom and I agreed to move on to the next place called Uncles. It was a much larger club, and they had several pool tables and darts—and it was loud with our type of music. It was only a few more blocks down College Avenue on the same side of the street.

As we got close to the entrance of Uncles, I saw a bright-red car in the front of the bar. A bright-red beautiful Mustang Coup. It was a fine car with a gorgeous girl sitting on the curbside passenger's seat close to us. Her window was wide open. She sat alone with no one else in the car. It looked like she was waiting for someone inside Uncles. We were turning to go up the steps to Uncles when I heard Bob loudly yell, "I would love to jump that girl."

I now could feel the blood rushing to my face from the embarrassment. I turned around immediately and pointed my finger at Bob's face as I looked up at him. "Just keep your mouth shut."

His reply was "Awe, she never heard me."

I reminded him again to "just shut up if you want to go along with us again." Up the stairs we bounded, and into the bar we went.

We now entered and this one was packed even more than the last one. We downed several more beers, waiting to use the pool tables. Bob was still close to us, which made it difficult to talk to any of the girls. I felt we were losing valuable time, and Bob was not helping at all after several attempts with the ladies.

Finally, we could use the pool tables. We played a few games, drank a few more beers, and spent some time there. We now decided it was time to head to another hot spot before we started to find our way back to the house.

Feeling the beers as well as a few shots, we slowly walked toward another place on the same side of the street. It was not long, and I heard a set of tires screaming to a halt ever so close to us. I feared that the car was close enough to hit one of us.

As I jumped in fear and turned around, I wanted to see if we were going to get hit by the car. There it was, the same bright red shiny Mustang car we'd seen the girl sitting in at the last place. This time, out jumped four of the biggest guys I had ever seen. Each one was well over two hundred pounds. I saw one of the guys jump out of the car and yell, "Let's Get them!"

Bob, with his long legs, took off running down the middle of the street away from all of us. He ran so fast, there was no catching him. He quickly lost them after running down the ally and over several blocks. They were big, but not fast. These big muscle heads were not built for speed. He had left us there to fight alone. It was now four against two. Tom and I each tried to run, but we were quickly caught on the sidewalk by the guys in the red car. Bob was long gone by now, since we lived about eight blocks from our present location.

Tom now received several punches and kicks as he was quickly brought to the ground. Two of the guys took turns punching on him once he was down. Kicking him relentlessly. As soon as he hit the ground, they kicked him over and over. I could hear him groan in pain. One guy had me pressed up against the wall tight with his huge hand at my neck lifting upward.

When they were done with Tom, he was out cold and bloody. All four were now in front of me. As the one held my head tight against the brick wall, the one behind him proclaimed, "Yea, she said this is the one that said it."

I started to say "Wait" when the first blow hit me hard in the forehead. Before I could say anything again, I saw the large fist again with a huge class ring headed toward my face. I was up against a brick wall, and I could feel my head get pounded the first few times, and then it was over. One guy held my arms so I could not swing back to defend myself.

I never knew how many times they hit me because I now lay on the sidewalk, passed out. A short time went by as I came to again. I heard voices while one eye was tightly closed. I could now see several people around Tom trying to get him up as my face lay close to the cement sidewalk. Tom's face was bloody and swollen. He mumbled in pain as he tried to lift himself up.

I tried to get myself up but could not do it. My legs would not respond. Several people were pulling me up, assisting me. Someone said they had called for an ambulance and it should be here soon. I was told to not move and to wait instead, but I wanted to get out of the area as soon as I could. I slowly crawled over to Tom, and we both started to help each other get up and move away from the crowd. I did not want to deal with the police either because I had just started the new job only a few months ago. I was sure also the guys that had just beat us up could come right back.

Tom and I helped each other through the ally toward our house. I could hardly speak, and I thought my jaw was broken now, and it hurt so bad. I knew it did not close properly.

We returned to the house after staggering our way back. Tom went directly to the bathroom to bandage his wounds. We entered the living room, and there was Bob, lying stretched out, relaxing on the couch, watching the Bucks basketball game. He saw us come in and acted like nothing happened.

Smiling, he said, "What took you guys so long?"

I wanted to jump on him and start teaching him a lesson, but the two other guys stopped me. The anger got worse and worse.

I heard Bob say again, "What took you guys so long to get back home?" Laughing as he said it. The other guys held me back again. They said, "He is slow and doesn't know any better. Let it go."

It took several weeks before I could close my mouth all the way. Eating was very difficult since I could not open my mouth enough. My boss at the shop asked me what happened when he saw several large cuts on my face, along with the large bumps on my forehead. He also could tell my speech was labored when I tried to talk with customers.

It took me several weeks before I would go out on College Avenue again to the local watering holes and clubs. I was sure those guys would spot me, and it would all start again. Never would I let Bob go with us after that, no matter what.

I learned to accept Bob and even played basketball with him on several occasions. He was just one of the guys that came and went from Independent House.

I remained in Appleton for over a year and then moved back to Random Lake to the town where I went to high school. I would finish my apprenticeship at a shop there.

CHAPTER #10

The Search

It had been fifteen years now since I had seen my real mother. Dennis and I wanted to find out where she was. I wondered if she would still know who I was if we found her? Karen lived in Milwaukee on the east side in a beautiful neighborhood. She'd become a very successful real estate agent and told us where Mother was living. We were told that real aunts and uncles lived up in that area also. I was anxious to search them out.

I learned that my real mother lived in Barron, Wisconsin only a few miles from where I was born. To my surprise, my foster parents encouraged Dennis and me to go forward and find her. We planned the trip and brought two of our close friends along. We would make it a long camping weekend and not rush anything.

We found Barron Wisconsin and drove into town with excitement. I asked myself over and over if she would know me. We first thought we knew where she might be, but there was no one living there. Next, we stopped at the local gas station and asked if they knew of any Jacksons in town. They did not know them either.

We next stopped at the local grocery store to get a snack and a soda. I casually asked the clerk if she had ever heard of anyone by the name of Jacksons in town or in the area. She remembered that two people by that name lived only a few blocks just west from the store we were at. She said it was a small yellow house that we could not miss if we went the few blocks down the street. It was located on the corner.

The excitement started to get intense as we hopped back into the car. They were the best words I could have heard. We were now so close to finding her.

We found the little yellow house just as described by the clerk. We stopped directly in front of it. Dennis and I discussed how we should introduce ourselves. It had been so many years since we saw her. We were confused as to how we should handle it. Our two friends waited in the car.

Dennis and I walked slowly to the front door, stepping up a few steps on the porch. I looked at Dennis as I knocked on the front door. My legs were now shaking. First, there was no response, but I thought I heard voices from within. I tried again, and a small woman came to the door, slowly opening it. She was a frail woman with dark brown hair and red, red lipstick. Before I could say anything, the little lady asked if we were door-to-door salesmen. Before I could say anything, she announced, "I don't want anything," and the door slammed shut in my face.

I looked at Dennis again and said, "I think that was her, Dennis. I really think that was her."

He told me to knock again. I knocked even louder than the first time, and the same little women came to the door again. She told me again that she did not want anything, and before she could close the door again in my face, I asked her if she was Mrs. Jackson.

"Yes," she said. "What do you want?"

With tears in my eyes, I slowly tried to speak. I started to tell her, "I think we are your sons."

She said nothing for a moment as the tears welled up in her eyes too. She hesitated and then realized who stood before her. She swung the doors wide open and reached out, crying and grabbing both of us with her arms spread open. Pulling us ever close, she yelled, "Mother, come quick. It's my boys!"

She now recognized us. Grandmother would have a hard time moving fast because she was in her late eighty's, and she walked slowly with a cane. Surprisingly, she was alive too. Mother and Grandmother together surprised Dennis and me both.

I now felt awkward telling her who I was and the families Dennis and I lived with about one hundred and fifty miles away.

We explained to her that we had our friends with us on our little trip and they were in the car. She invited them in as we talked for a period of time. The conversation was light - where we lived, our families, and how we were doing. She and Grandmother were not prepared for us, and I knew it was uncomfortable for them to discuss the past. I could also see very well what the situation was here.

Grandmother was in a role reversal and taking care of her daughter even in her advanced age, instead of Mother taking care of Grandmother. It was sad to see, but Mother had contracted throat cancer and become a dependent on alcohol also. Grandmother would purchase the alcohol by the case like people purchased soda. Mother got through the day with large amounts of alcohol. She would wake up and grab the bottle next to her bed, and she would set it down when she went to bed. It was her way of dealing with her cancer and various other problems from the past. I saw several cases in the tiny house.

It would be a few month later, I saw Mother at my brother Leo's house in Milwaukee. He and his wife Ellen now took care of her. Grandmother had passed away, and Leo and Ellen now took over the care.

MaryAnn and I were planning to get married in early August. I wanted my fiancé to meet Mother before the big day came. Leo had informed me that Mother was getting bad and it would not be long now according to the doctors, because of the throat cancer.

The doctor informed Mother that she needed a throat operation and she could extend her life a few more years. She refused and wanted the little insurance to go to us kids.

I was always glad I went to find her, to see her one more time. To let her know I was all right and I would be fine in the future. I had time to tell her I still loved her and missed her dearly. She passed away only a few months before I got married that year.

———

I got married on August 7, 1971, on one of the hottest days of the year. It was ninety five degrees, and we sweated it out in the little country church that was not air conditioned.

I quit the barbering shortly after. I got to hate it because it was too boring for me. Each day we talked about the weather fifty times or discussed the Packers Football team over and over, if not the Brewers. It seemed too confining to me.

CHAPTER # 11

Changing Careers

I wanted to get out and be with more people and experience more of the world. I decided to go and work in a factory because I could make more money than I did in the barbershop. I could also work with several of my friends at the factory.

A few years passed, and we had two little boys Brian and Bradley. The excitement was great since we were close to my work also. We purchased a small house in Grafton, Wisconsin. It was a small three-bedroom house in town, and the cost of $17,000 dollars only. We both had jobs, and mine was only about ten blocks from where our house was. The company I worked for now was Tecumseh Engine company. When I was not at home, I was across the street from my house working on cars with my good friend Dennis Kohlmier. We became lifelong friends. He was a Volkswagen expert, and we took engines in and out. We also did a lot of repair work on them in his garage that doubled as a workshop.

I started at the new company as a small drill-press operator, nothing too big, but I was happy to have a regular job. I soon moved up to a machinist position. That meant machining heavy crankshafts and blocks with coolant flying all over. I worked for a while on that job, and I learned that the guy who came around each hour to inspect my parts had a much more relaxing and clean job. He usually stayed cleaner than me. He also did not get so exhausted from bending over the large boxes .These held crankshafts that were not only heavy but cumbersome. The big boxes were moved from location to location for machining with a lift truck. His title was line Inspector. He came around once every hour. I soon wanted that job and applied for it.

I studied blueprint reading, tools, and as much as I could to qualify to be an inspector. It was only after only a few months of working there that I got the line inspector job.

Next, I moved on to where they built carburetors. It was a clean airconditioned room. Rows and rows of women drilling, stamping, pressing, and turning out many different pieces for the small engines, mostly carburetors. It was great to get out of the dirty shop and into a clean job again.

After several years, the layoffs started to happen. I found I did not have enough seniority to keep the nice clean job. Anyone with more time could request my position. Before I got laid off, I found myself back in the dirty machine shop, milling large engine blocks and coolant spraying all over. Getting soaked feet daily was not my idea of a good day.

The machine shop job lasted just over nine years, and many of our jobs were being shipped out of the country to Mexico. My foreman always said that I had nothing to worry about if I had nine years of seniority. That day finally did arrive, and my name was at the top of the list to be laid off.

MaryAnn and I had adopted a little girl while she was several months pregnant. The baby was only a few months old when we took her in as a foster child. She was at our house for six months, and the agency informed us that she would be adopted out soon. We had grown so attached to her, and we were ready to go to court to keep her. We both agreed that she was part of our family now.

The court date soon came, and we carried our little girl into court with us. The wait was not long, and soon the judge called us up front. He then looked at the paperwork for us to keep her or adopt her out to someone else. He asked one question: "What name would you call this little girl?"

Her name would be Mellissa Sue Jackson.

The judge then said, "That's a beautiful name." And he signed the adoption papers for us to keep her. Out the door of the courthouse, we went. A few months later, we had our fourth child. It was a little girl we named Michelle. With two girls and two boys, our family was complete. MaryAnn and I started to take in several foster children over the next ten years. Some called us mom and dad for several years after they left us. I got phone calls from several calling me Pops. Even after years of being out on their own.

————

I wanted to purchase a collector car I had always wanted back in high school. I was looking for a 1957 Chevrolet Bel-Air in any condition. Another employee from another department saw my request on the bulletin board and told me he had one. He stated he was in an unusual position while owning this car. I asked him, "What do you mean by that?"

"Well, this is my predicament. My aunt is holding the car hostage over in her garage! When I purchased the car several years ago, I had no money, and my dad and my aunt helped me with half of money to purchase it. I paid my dad back but never paid his sister, my aunt. She informed my dad to get that car over to her house until I paid her. My dad then brought it over to her house, and she locked it in her garage. That is where it has sat for several years."

My next big question was "How much do you owe her?"

He said, "You can have the car for what I owe her, and that is three hundred dollars only." I considered the price and figured it must be rusty and damaged at that price, but I wanted to see it and purchase if possible. I knew I wanted a 57 Chevrolet.

We agreed to meet in the town his aunt lived in to check it out the following Saturday morning. I arrived at the agreed time of 10:00 a.m. with my checkbook in my back pocket, along with my friend from near home. The guy selling the car arrived about the same time I did. His aunt came out of the house as soon as he was out of his car.

"You're not taking that car until you pay me!" she shouted. He explained to her that I had to check it out first or inspect it before I decided to purchase it. She went over to the front of the garage. Bending over, she unlocked the big door. She then pulled up the garage door open for me to see. I now got the shakes because he'd never told me it was a convertible. He'd never mentioned that it was in beautiful condition. It was a bright-red car with a white soft top. It had the black and silver interior. It even had the correct hubcaps and wheel skirts still on it with not a spot of damage. Only a little rust on the front bumper.

I immediately told him I would buy it. I pulled the checkbook out of my back pocket. I could tell I was shaking as I scribbled out the check to her. My friend and I brought it home immediately. One flat tire on the way home did not bother me.

After approximately forty-five collector cars, I still love every one of them. I am always looking for the next one to restore. I had worked on many to get them to car shows all over Wisconsin. At first, I was just happy just to attend and then working to win the Best of Show trophy. Some turned out being restored so fine or rare that they could be easily found on Google as examples of fine classic cars in that make or rarity.

After Tecumseh notified us about the upcoming layoffs, I was called to the office and notified the layoff would be for at least three to four years before I would be called back. If I wanted to get another job, they would understand my situation. I hated to leave that job, since many of my friends were there, and I lived close by.

I worked a few security jobs in the area to keep some money coming in.

We talked it over at home and both agreed that a fulltime job was the only way we could get by. I now searched the papers weekly as to what kind of jobs were available. I sent out resumes daily. After some time, I decided to see what other people had to say in the "work wanted" section of the paper. I saw the usual description of what kind of college degrees, courses, and training they had. Along with that, the usual description of what type of job they were looking for. I thought about it for a day or so and decided I wanted to stand out from the other usual ads. I wanted something they would notice right away. I wrote an ad up several times and tossed them each into the trash basket, trying to write a catchy ad. Maybe someone would notice my ad over the rest. After writing what I thought was a clever ad, I decided to give the Milwaukee Journal "work wanted" department a call.

I requested that the lady not laugh when she was ready to write down my ad. I informed her I wanted the first few lines to have only two big bold words on top: "Mr. Personality looking for sales job, sales representative, or an opportunity to get into sales."

I added that I was a machinist, could read blueprints, sold autos, and was eager to work with a positive attitude.

She now giggled and read it back to me. She gave me the price, and I eagerly waited to see if I would get a response. Searching each night for my ad in the next few daily papers. It would be only a few weeks before I got laid off, and I thought I had nothing to lose with this ad I was placing.

After only a few days had passed, and I discovered my ad in the paper. It was not long, and I started to get some phone calls. Then, a few days into the next week brought several letters in the mail. A few with offers to interview. I now was proud of my attempt to get a new job and the ad I had made up.

One such phone call brought a great opportunity, I thought. It was a machine shop in Milwaukee that had called me. It was about forty miles south of where I lived. The gentlemen on the other end of the phone said he had a position they were creating at their company. They were looking for someone like myself to fill it. He asked if I could come down to Milwaukee and talk with him about it.

I said, "Yes, of course," and he told me the time and location. He would have his general manager talk to me about the possible job when I got there. It was a sales position, and it covered the lower half of Wisconsin.

Milwaukee being miles south of where I lived in the country, I knew the company was on the near northeast side of downtown Milwaukee, just off North Avenue. I nervously searched out the company address. I had planned to have lots of time to find it, so I had left home plenty early, and I was happy I did.

I soon arrived at a white building that took up half of the block. It was a two-story company that had the parking lot across the street. Several large yellow box trucks were in a fenced-in yard. It was situated in primarily a rough neighborhood, and I was eager to find out what they did as a business in this area.

The office was upstairs, and the secretary had me take a seat in a small waiting room while I waited for the owner. Soon, an older gentleman came out with papers in his hands, a big smile on his face. He eagerly invited me into his office. I found myself sitting directly in front of his big desk. He now lifted the newspaper to look at my resume on his desk.

"So, you are Mr. Personality. I have never seen an ad like that before," he said.

I replied, "I sure am. And I will be the best salesperson you have ever had."

"You're pretty sure of yourself," he said. He then read my short resume aloud. I could see he had circled my ad in the newspaper that lay on his desk.

"What do you know about field machining?" he asked.

I replied to him, "Not a thing, sir, but I can learn"

"That's good. I like to hear that," he came back.

After several questions about my qualifications, where I lived, and possible salary offered, he asked when I could start. I told him I had a few days left at the engine company but could start that following Monday. He then brought me into the general manager's office to give me the final details of my responsibility.

I found out I would be offered a new company car, a salary for the first time that exceeded what I was making in the factory by several thousand dollars, and an expense account. How could I say no? I was informed that I would be expected to go out and look for work for our crews or jobs for the company to do inside our machine shop.

It was a field machining company that sent out crews to do repairs for other companies. The machine shop assisted the crews that went out on each repair. They designed equipment with a few engineers to do large jobs on-site that companies could not handle themselves.

The job was very exciting because it took me all over. First, in Wisconsin then in Illinois, Iowa, and Minnesota. I mentioned that I wanted to find all kinds of work for us.

The owner told me to "keep going. The less we see you, the better."

Jobs started coming in on a regular basis. It was only a few months, and it all would be working out well. After a few months, I was called into the general manager's office. I was a bit nervous when he told me to "come right in; I want to talk to you about your expense reports." I now felt my nerves in my legs and chest.

I slowly walked into his office, and I could see the pile of receipts I had turned in with my reports. He started to read some of them off to me. "Motel $35.00, McDonalds $3.25, Burger King $4.00, and another motel at $39.00. This has to stop right now!" he exclaimed, and I became very nervous. I had thought I was being very careful with the company's money because it was not mine.

He said with concern in his voice, "From now on, you will eat in the best restaurants you can find. You will stay in the best hotels or motels in the area. No more cheap ones. If you want to take customers out to eat, you have to eat in the best places you can get into. Also, feel free to buy drinks if the situation depends on it, and last, you can fly to locations farther away. It doesn't pay for you to drive for three days and spend a day or two and drive three days back. Just let the receptionist know where you want to go. She will make the arrangements for you. Just tell her your schedule for where you want to go."

I left the meeting feeling like I now had the go ahead to really show them what I could do to improve and increase sales. I would go further, start more trade shows, and spend more time training new representatives at different locations throughout the United States. I explained, I wanted to make reps and make them into a group of little Jacksons to do what I had done over the past year. The owner agreed to go ahead with my plans, but I would be totally responsible to keep them busy. I also would make up the contract for them and get the final approval from the owner of the company.

I soon made up an easy contract to present to the representative I started. The owner and general manager agreed that it was a fine agreement to move ahead. Sales were starting to boom.

After a few years, I requested to expand all over the country, starting a marketing department that included trade show displays at shows in every industry we now were capable of working. We went after work in the mining industry, large shipping, power plants, steel plants, foundries, and any other large industrial plants. I soon scheduled fifteen trade shows a year and sent the displays to each location. My budget grew to a quarter million a year in marketing alone, but the sales were skyrocketing from doing it. I organized the reps to assist at each show in their area from Florida, Massachusetts, and California, plus several other states.

We now competed for work with companies like General Electric and Westinghouse, and others. We did large repairs of generators and steam turbines. Our crews did work in some of the largest steel mills and manufacturing plants in the United States. I set up a network of representatives around the country. Twenty-five new locations with contracts. They would find the work like I did when I started. I provided them the training and gave them a ton of literature to use. Each industry had its own set of literature, and it worked out fine for several years. They would answer to me as the director of sales and marketing in my new capacity. Of course, the owner of our company had the last say on anything.

I found myself planning trips almost weekly. There were trade shows, inspections for repairs, and training for the reps, along with time for my group of reps I had acquired over several months.

———

Over the years that I worked at the machining company, I met many nice people all over the country. I experienced a lot of strange things in many places from New York; Miami; Portland, Oregon; Los Angeles, California; and Toronto, Canada.

On one occasion, while doing a tradeshow in Atlanta, Georgia, I decided to go to a local dance club and have a few drinks and check the place out. The rep I was working with suggested we go to this place after having dinner in a fine restaurant in town.

As soon as we entered the place, I could feel my pants vibrating due to the loud music. The heavy beat was great, and the show band on stage looked fine. The group consisted of guitars, several brass horns, a drummer, a keyboard guy, and a sax man. The dance floor was packed, and everyone danced like there was no tomorrow. I knew we had come to the right place.

With three large bars in the place, I quickly walked over to the one nearest to my left. I squeezed past a few people to get close to the bar. I ordered a mug of beer and looked around to check out the place. It was a high-class club with a second-floor restaurant that had a glass wall toward the dance floor. People stood close to the glass to see the action down on the dance floor.

So many were in the restaurant and on the dance floor. I had never been in such a big club before.

Soon I notice several people heading toward the main door I had just come through. The excitement was building as a large group pushed toward the door, closer and closer.

Straining to see what was happening, I tried to see over the crowd from the bar area. It was a lady coming in with what I thought was a monkey on her shoulder. I could not believe she was bringing her pet monkey into this classy club.

She seemed to have an entourage close and around her.

As she got closer to our bar, the crowd was getting louder. I could see it was not a monkey at all but a small kid hanging onto her shoulder. Why would she come into this place with a kid, and who was he? As she got closer to our bar, I could plainly see that was not just a kid either, but a real man. No ordinary man, but the world's smallest man, as the bartender explained why they were there. He told me they were here for a photo shoot. The man she held was in the Guinness World Book of Records as the smallest man in the world.

She set him up on the bar, and he slowly moved down toward where I was sitting. Everyone wanted to shake his hand or touch him. He was shaking hands with several patrons and handing out a few autographs. When he got in front of me, he grabbed my mug of beer with both of his little hands. One on each side. He slowly lifted it, and I could see it was heavy for him as he raised it to his mouth and emptied it. Everyone let out a cheer.

Everyone wanted to get close and touch him. The media people continued to take pictures. When the band had finished with the present song, the little guy's entourage moved toward the stage. She held him on her shoulder again as they moved through the crowd.

She set him on the stage, and a guy in charge started to arrange the set they wanted for the next photos. He told the midget to stand near the saxophone for that special shot. The midget walked over to the sax and stood directly under it as it rested on the stand. He was short enough to fit under it, and I thought that was neat, as did the others. The cheering continued with each photo taken. Flashes also went on and on for several minutes from the crowd.

The time came to leave after the photo shoot. They would leave in a hurry to their next appearance or location. They jumped into a big limousine at the curb. I had just witnessed something I could hardly get my head around. I asked myself if I'd just seen what I really saw? It was something I would never forget.

It was mid-August in 1985 when I was scheduled to attend a large trade show in Los Angeles. I had my secretary put me at the Figueroa Hotel not far from Hollywood. I knew I could go and check out all popular spots I had heard about and seen at the movies and on TV. I was close enough to drive to several locations and even see the homes of several stars. I proceeded to see the Queen Mary, The Spruce Goose, and several other things. I walked and saw all the big-named stars on the Hollywood Walk of Fame, along with lots of famous places like Capital Records and Universal Studios.

I got to LA early enough to meet my representative. We made sure our display for the show was set up and ready on time. All the literature was in place, and it would look impressive to the several thousand that would attend this show. The show would last three days at one of the largest convention centers. I always arrived a few days before the show. I did this so I could make several sales calls with the representative in that area.

It was one of these evenings. We got back early, and I thought I would venture out on the town. I went to the concierge to ask if there were any good clubs in the area. He suggested a few I might be interested in, and one caught my attention. He claimed it was but a few minutes away by car in Hollywood—or I could take a taxi if I wanted him to call for one. He claimed it was very popular and would be crowded later. He suggested I get their early.

I knew I was not familiar with driving in the area, so I chose to take the taxi. It arrived in a few minutes, and off we went to Hollywood. We arrived at the location, and I paid the driver. As I turned to look at the place, I could see it was not located on the ground floor. It was on the second floor, where all the lights were flashing out the windows, and I could hear the loud music playing from the sidewalk.

I walked up the stairs and found the nightclub's main entrance. It was very high class with a nice big bar. It had a large dance floor that I could see held many people. This was no club like I had ever seen in Wisconsin.

I sat at one of the many tables around the dance floor and started to have a few drinks. The atmosphere was hopping, and it felt good to relax after a busy day calling on customers.

I must have been there a few hours, and I thought I would ask one of the beautiful ladies to dance. What could it hurt? I asked myself. These were not farm girls, like in Wisconsin where I lived, but girls in Hollywood, California.

I picked out a lady that I thought might be alone. She had raven-black hair, and I could see she knew how to dance very well. When I got up the nerve, I proceeded in her direction. I arrived at her table while she sat with a few other lady friends.

The song was a slower one. I was nervous, but I wanted to dance at least once. I knew I should not hold her too tightly because I was a stranger. I would try to talk with her and just be friendly. She seemed very shy and did not say much, and I could tell she was a bit uncomfortable as we danced.

As the music came to an end, I thanked her and walked back to my table, and she returned to hers also. It lasted only a few minutes, and I felt dumb at my feeble attempt. I decided that I would just sit and observe the rest dancing and drink for the rest of the evening only.

I sat at my table after the dance for only a few minutes when I felt a tap on my shoulder.

"You're not from around here are you?" a voice from the rear of me asked. As I turned to see who it was, I said "Did I dance that bad?"

Not knowing a soul in this place, I wondered who was asking me here.

He then said, "You don't know who you were dancing with either, do you?"

"No," I replied, hoping it was not his girlfriend. I did not want to get into a fight. He told me his name as he pulled out his wallet. He then proceeded to show me his badge. His badge told me he was an FBI agent. A feeling of despair came over me. What now? I thought. What did I get myself into now?.

He then asked me to look back at the girl I had just danced with. "Do you notice anything unusual about her? Do you see all the guys hanging around behind her?"

I replied, "Yes, I do now. I did not notice before you said anything"

He explained that there were a few other officers in the club. They were there to keep a lookout on the girl and those guys around her. He explained that the girl was the daughter of one of LA's biggest cocaine importers.

"We know he flies in several helicopters a year. We have to keep an eye on those guys in case any deals might go down."

"It's good you did not do anything stupid with her on the dance floor like grabbing her, or one of those guys would have probably hurt you. They may have taken you out the back door. We know they are here to watch over her. They are bodyguards hired by her father."

I laughed a little, relieved. The ice was now broken.. I told him why I was in town and how I came to be here tonight. He told me that he had relatives in Madison, Wisconsin and that he got back to Wisconsin on occasion. He made me feel more comfortable as we talked.

Of course, I had to tell him of my hobby of old cars. I informed him that I would take a classic car that was not too bad and restore it to show condition. I explained I learned to love all types of cars. He then asked if I'd parked my car in the regular parking lot or the other one.

"No," I said. "I took a taxi here."

"You are going to love this then." We left the dance floor and went to the garage area.

As we entered the regular garage, and he said, "This is where the regular people park."

All the cars were the usual family type—Chevrolets, Fords, Buicks, Toyotas, and others. Then he brought me to another side of the garage. As he opened the door, my eyes could only look in amazement at the autos it held within.

He said, "This is where the rich kids park."

All I could see were Ferraris, Lamborghinis, Porsches, Mercedes, and many other expensive cars. They even had security guards just to watch over them.

The detective and I parted company, and I thanked him for tapping me on the shoulder.

I stayed until closing and stood on the sidewalk, waiting for my taxi. I had to see all those expensive and fancy cars leave the garage area. It was like a car show for me as, one by one, they exited the garage. One more fantastic than the next. I knew I would not forget this for a long time. It was a strange and beautiful night in Hollywood.

———

Along with the many good and unusual times on the job, I also learned to handle the hard times. It was one of these times I was called to the owner's office. He was extremely excited as I entered. I was in a great mood also. I had just gotten a contract signed for a large job in Pennsylvania. It would take a crew of ten men working around the clock several weeks to finish the repair. Easily it will be billed out at $100,000 or more.

He shook my hand and said, "What a good job," as I sat down. He then referred me to the big jobs we had done in the past for Union Electric in St. Louis and how they were such good customers.

I knew we did a few jobs because I was the first person to call on Union Electric for work. None too big, I recalled. All the owner could say was "How good we are" and "What good work we do.

"They like us," he said with pride.

With that said, he asked me to arrange to go back to them and see if we could get some more work. It had been several months since we did any work for them, and he was sure they would have more for us to do.

I went to my office and got on the phone right away to contact the purchasing department. I had several contacts there, and surly I could get in within the next several days. The receptionist answered at the phone at Union Electric and connected me to my contact in purchasing. Not sounding very friendly, he agreed that he would see me on Tuesday morning at 10:00 a.m. the following week. It was short, and he hung up.

Excited, I went home for the weekend, knowing I would be off to St. Louis on Monday morning. Early Monday morning came, and I was headed to St. Louis. I had packed for several days and planned for a week of sales calls on the road.

After another night in the same old hotel setting, I made sure I was up early for my appointment at Union Electric. I always arrived early to purchasing for these appointments. I never wanted to be a second late. The receptionist was cordial when I told her I had an appointment with Mr. Walker in purchasing. She made a phone call and then said to me, "They are in the conference room waiting for you, Mr. Jackson."

I reminded her my appointment was only with Mr. Walker. She answered another phone call and did not respond. Now she asked me to "have a seat please. They will we right with you."

I sat and waited to be called in. After a short wait, the receptionist informed me that I could proceed into the conference room down the hall. "They are ready to see you now, Mr. Jackson."

In I went, and as soon as the conference door opened, I could see a long table where five people sat on each side, along with a gentleman at the far end. This truly was not what I was expecting. One chair remained open for me.

I did not know why all these people were in the room, and my immediate response was to pull out those calling cards and beam, friendly, saying, "Hello, I'm Bruce Jackson from On-site Machining Company."

Quickly the man at the end of the long table stood up and yelled in an angry voice, "We all know who you are, Mr. Jackson, and who your company is. Have a seat!"

No one in the room dared utter a word.

I quickly sat down in the last available seat at the far end from where the angry guy was standing. As I learned, the angry man was the director of purchasing and manager of accounting. He sat at the far end of the table. He had a large pile of papers in front of him as he stood up. He then lifted the pile of papers high into the air.

"Who the hell do you people think you are?" he yelled it in my direction. "You people will never work for us again or any other power plant in the country if I can help it!"

He now threw the pile of papers onto the table. They scattered everywhere. Flying into the air and floating to the floor. Several people in the room gasped and sat back into their chairs with amazement.

Never had I seen someone so angry and red in the face. He directed his anger right at me now. "You people tell us the job is going to cost us $30,000 and you send us a bill for $94,500? What do you have to say about this, Mr. Jackson?"

A cold sweat now covered my body. I tried to open my mouth as they all stared directly at me. I told him I would check into it since it came from our billing department.

He then said, "You do that. Now get out of here. All of you."

All the purchasing staff shuffled out one at a time. After they were all out the door, I followed last. I felt so defeated knowing I was set up by the owner of our company. These people were waiting for me.

I knew there were public phones in the lobby downstairs. We had no personal portable phones yet. I was shaking as I rode the elevator down to the main floor. My legs trembled as I made my way to the phones on the wall.

I knew I was set up ahead of time. I knew they had already called our billing department and talked with our owner about the final billing on several occasions. That's how it was done at our company. The owner always had the last word about pricing and the final bill. It had all happened when I was on the road looking for more work or at a tradeshow. I often was told to worry about getting in more sales and stay out of the billing department all together.

Our owner was sure that Mr. "Happy-Go-Lucky" Bruce could go in there and smooth it all out. Even get the check from the purchasing department and bring it back. That was why he'd been so gleeful in his office and eager to suggest I go into Union Electric in St. Louis in the first place the week before.

I finally crossed the lobby to the phones. My fingers struggled to find the numbers as I shook. Our receptionist in Milwaukee on the other end now connected me to the owner. The first words out of his mouth were "Hi, Bruce. How is it going? Do they have any more work for us?" As if he didn't know.

"Don't ever do this to me again! You set me up!" I shouted. I did not care at the time if I got fired. I was so angry myself. I informed him, "If you ever do this again to me, it will be my last day. They are angry as hell right now."

He then said the dumbest thing he could have said to me as I was shaking on the phone, "When do thy have any more work for us?" I then slammed the phone down on him. I knew I would not get anywhere discussing this matter.

I was required to call into the office daily to report in as to how it was going. I refused to call the office for the rest of the week. I wondered how it would go when I returned on Monday morning.

His response to these kind of problems was not working with the customers. He felt it was his job to just threaten the customer with lawyers. He would not come to a fair agreement or negotiate. He would inform the customers that he had fifty lawyers ready to go to court if he did not get paid. He claimed that the customer gave our quoting department a purchase order number to do the job, and the verbal quote meant nothing. It did not matter what our quoting department had told them it would cost. That was just verbal. This had all happened when I was constantly on the road, looking for more work for us to do.

Since I was the person who had found the jobs and I was the one who had direct contact with the customers, it became a chore working between the customers and our company. I knew our policies were causing most of the problems.

I would visit the owner's office on many occasions. I would plead with him and tell him, "Our sales are being hurt, and we'd better change the way we do business right away!"

His response was always the same: "Just find the work, Bruce. That's your job, and we will handle the rest."

On one occasion, I got to a company, and the purchasing guy had pleaded for me to help him out. I had given him a price on a job from the quoting department, and our company had billed him totally different. He cried in front of me as he informed me his job was on the line. He asked if I could I help him out so he did not lose his position. It would happen again and again over the next several years. I would be in the middle with the customer and our company on the other side. Eventually there were several states I could not enter into any longer, and it was getting worse. The word was getting out in a lot of areas and industries.

After doing two big trade shows in a row, gone twelve days, I told the general manager I would like to take off a few days and spend them with the family. He picked up the phone to speak to the owner. I was then asked to go into the owner's office.

The owner instructed me then to look at the large pile of papers on his desk. "Do you know what that pile of papers on my desk is, Bruce?"

"No," I said.

"It is a large group of people looking for your job! So, get out there and do it."

I left his office, feeling totally frustrated. How much more could I do?

At one time, while venturing out, I went to see a few companies in upper Wisconsin and the Upper Peninsula of Michigan, and I ran into a problem with my company car. The rear end went out, and the car rolled to a stop about a hundred miles from our company. Fortunately, I was in a small little town, and the phone booth was not far. I walked for a while to reach it.

I called my company so I could get directions as to what they wanted to do next. Call a tow truck or what. It was then that I was informed by the receptionist to talk to the general manager. He was a squirrely little man that wore pink socks. I never cared for him because he knew little about our business and giggled with the girls all the time in the office.

He told me he did not know how to handle this situation, but he would talk to the owner as to how the company would handle it.

He soon came back on the phone. He said I should talk directly to the owner of the company about this. He then transferred me over to the owner's office. I knew the general manager had no backbone. His management skills were useless. I often wondered how he got his job.

The owner asked what was the matter, and I explained it again. He now inquired if I lived in the area or close to where I was broken down at the time? I Immediately told him, "No, I live about forty-five miles to the southwest."

He then told me to find someone to purchase the vehicle and bring the check back into the office on Monday. "What! You want me to sell it out here?" I asked. "Out here where I am ten miles from the next town?"

"Yes," he replied and hung up the phone on me.

Now, I was totally frustrated at my predicament. I thought how stupid it was for them to just abandon me here so far away.

I knew a few people close to my house that had a garage, but that was forty miles away. I'd brought my own car there on several occasions. I knew they had a small used car lot, and I put my plan into motion.

When I called the garage, I informed my friend who owned the garage that "the rear end went out on the car, and I am a good distance away. The car is only a few years old. It was always a great car. It had just under a hundred thousand miles and never let me down."

I also informed them that I would sell them the car for only fifty dollars. They would have to come and pick it up. It had to be paid with a check with our company name on it after he picked me up.

He laughed and asked, "Why are you selling it so cheap?"

I told him, "That's all I want because they left me out in the sticks! They never told me how much I should get for this car. Just sell it!" I knew it was a three-hundred-dollar repair, and I could be back on the road. It did not take long for the garage guys to arrive and tow it back to their shop.

I got dropped off at my house afterward, and I received the check. I knew that on Monday, when I returned to my office, there would be some excitement.

I went directly into the general manager's office with the check. He looked at it and grumbled about how small it was. I could see him scoot into the owner's office. I left his office and went to my office, laughing all the way.

The next day, I was at the big dealership looking at another new company car to purchase. The general manager gave me a check for the full amount, and I picked up my new car. They knew that I was a great salesmen and our success was depending on it.

CHAPTER #12

Lessons Learned

Many problems came up like this over the next several years. As I tried to settle the disputes with the customers, it also got more and more difficult to settle things with the representatives I had placed around the country. It was a constant battle. I found myself in the middle all the time. Often I had one or another rep call me and tell me they did not get their commissions for the work. Some would quit, and others just stopped looking for work.

The owner continually told me that it was my job to keep the work coming in. It was my job to keep the now fifty guys in the shop, those on the road, and all the office people working daily. The pressure was really on.

The job grew slowly in salary also. The frustrations became more constant. Soon nepotism on the owner's part creeped into the company when his two sons graduated from school. Soon the owner did not want to pay the money owed to the reps even if we had a good contract with them. He claimed it was too much money to just give away. They too brought in some big jobs. It became a large part of my life trying to settle arguments on contracts and continually hiring new reps. Others would just quit, disgruntled at the constant fighting with the owner.

I spent a lot of time away from home, and I sacrificed so much time with my children. Sometimes weeks at a time. It took its toll, and as eleven years on the job came and went, I decided it was time for me to give it all up. We had grown from only a few hundred thousand dollars a year when I started to topping ten million dollars a year. My wife had put up with a lot over the years, and it was understandable when the divorce papers came. I could now admit that success was not worth it. Somehow coming from nothing to staying in the finest hotels and getting new cars and eating in the finest places in New York, San Francisco, and Miami, along with all the travel, had done more harm than good.

Coming from nothing as a small boy, I continually tried to show the owners how successful I could be. How many sales I could get in and how much more money we could bring in. I knew no one could stop me from doing this difficult job, but forgot the most important things in my life like family and friends. Now with even the success, I felt more and more alone. I wanted to be accepted, and I'd thought being a great salesmen would do it.

After eleven years at the machining company I decided to quit it all and do something else. I had his kid in my sales department trying to tell me what to do his first day on the job, and he knew nothing about the business. His dad, the owner, wanted me to teach his son everything about the business and how I'hadd build it up as he patted me on the back. His son told me that he was going to be my boss soon, according to his dad. I told him to look on my desk and read what the sign on my desk said; it read, "Bruce Jackson, Director of Sales and Marketing."

"My name will be on there in a few weeks," his son said. I knew what was coming.

I went into the owner's office and informed the owner that it was "called nepotism." I informed him I would take my vacation pay and be done with my job at the end of the week. He pleaded with me to stay on for only a few more months to train his son, but I could clearly see there was no appreciation for the success or sacrifice I had made over the past eleven years. I would leave this company on my own terms.

———

I went out on my own for several years and represented several companies. I now lived on the west side of Milwaukee. Karen did not live far from me, and it was nice to have her close. I traveled north to Green Bay to see my brother Leo on occasion also. His family lived a few miles north of Green Bay. He became a great carpenter and even did work on Lambeau Field, where the Packers played. When it was remodeled and expanded, he was part of the carpenters union that did the work. He was so proud of the work he did. He would explain it all to me when I went over to his house. Each countertop, each storage area, and the detailed work he had to do. He was a talented carpenter and proud of the fine work he did.

———

Later, when I was a regional rep for a tank company in Minnesota, work would bring me to a small town called Beaver Dam, Wisconsin. It was located about forty-five miles northwest

of Milwaukee. I lived alone and traveled for work as a representative for one main company and a few small others. That
was until things got slow in the economy. The cost and expenses
were taking up a lot of money because I was totally independent.
It was getting harder and harder to make ends meet, so I started
looking again at what I could do now at an age nearly fifty. No
one wanted to hire an older man to be a regional sales manager,
when there were so many young guys out there who would work
for less and run hard.

CHAPTER #13

A New Beginning

I soon searched the papers again. Very few jobs were available, and most wanted the guys with degrees or younger guys.

I had heard from someone that the state prison systems were always looking for someone to work in the prisons. It sounded crazy to me because this was so far different from what I'd been doing the past twenty years and most of my life. I found out when and where they were going to have their next interviews. It would be in Oshkosh, Wisconsin, at the University of Wisconsin campus.

I waited for my turn to talk to some of the captains who were there doing interviews. I asked them if I was too old for this.

They replied, "Oh hell, no! We have lots of guys your age and older. One explained that I would have to pass the six-week training program to see if I could be accepted first. It included state laws, physical-condition tests, and rules and regulations on how to handle inmates. He said he could sign me up right away if I wanted. They would also have to do a background check on me before I would be notified by the state to be accepted into the next training class. I signed right up, anxious to go to work full time.

I waited for the letter from the state to arrive, and after several weeks, it came. I spent the time exercising, running several miles a day, and quitting smoking. I knew this test would not be easy for me at my age.

The acceptance letter to attend classes finally came, and I knew this was my chance.

The training started, and each of us listened to the instructions intently. We received a larger volume of instructions and regulations to follow. We took these home to study.

I soon was sitting in a college classroom in Oshkosh. We also were doing all kinds of physical testing like I'd done in high school. It included pull ups, running, sit ups, and lots more. It was all on a timed basis according to your age. Most of the men and women were younger than me. The written tests on state law and other rules and regulations were weekly. After six weeks, a final exam on everything would determine if I could become an officer for the State of Wisconsin. The final exam would be long and took several hours.

Nightly I stayed awake to learn all the things I needed to. Sometimes until two in the morning. The final was coming in a hurry, and I wanted to score high on the test and get this job. If I did not, I could try again next year.

It was all over in a few hours, and the sweating was done. They collected the tests and we were instructed to come back the next day to hear the results. I returned on a Friday with the other ninety people applying. We were told to listen carefully to the results. First, they announced a bunch of names, and those people were instructed to move over to the next room. One by one, they called out about fifteen names. Each one arose and went to the next room.

We all sat still and wondered what was happening. After the last name was called, they announced that each of us had passed the tests. We were now all officers. We were all going to be attending a graduation ceremony.

The others did not make it. We all sighed with relief, and the assignments now took place. It was a lottery system. Each prison listed on a bulletin board up front would send in the number of officers they needed at the time. It could be one, three, or maybe even ten. The rule was that, if you were assigned to a prison, it was your obligation to work there for at least a year. No excuses. If you could not work at your assigned prison, you were dropped. You were allowed to try again in six months. All our names would be called out according to seniority. It depended on your age, if you had state time in another field, or the first letter of your last name. You were allowed to request your first three prisons of choice.

No matter where the prison was in the state, you got your first assignment. It did not matter if you even owned a home. Once you were assigned, you had to plan to serve your first full year there. You had to rent or make some type of arrangement. It did not matter if you lived several hundred miles from the prison you were picked for. Some even rented hotel rooms for a year. The only chance you had to work at a prison close to you was if there was one position available and you were called up next on the list. Some people who had passed the test quit on the spot if they did not get the prison they wanted in the selection. They would try again later.

Since I was one of the older people in the class, I had seniority over most of the class. I picked Waupun Correctional Facility in

Waupun, Wisconsin. It was an old Indian name for the town and prison. People called it Prison City, since there were three state prisons in the same town. One was a maximum prison, the one I was in was a medium/maximum, and the third was a minimum.

Ours was called a medium/maximum prison because all prisoners throughout the state came to us first to be processed. The minimum prison was the only one where inmates could go outside on a regular basis, and many had outside jobs, but they were required to return and check back in on a regular basis. Never were they gone more than eight hours at a time.

We maintained a regular population of inmates, like any other prison. Our population varied from eight hundred to twelve hundred inmates. Buses transported inmates on a daily basis throughout the state. The time at Dodge Correctional meant it was a period to adjust to where they were going depending on their sentence. Some had only a few years, and others had life in maximum without parole. They all had to come through our facility before they were sent on to one of the many prisons in the state. The only way that process would change would be if the inmate was considered a "high-priority" case.

There were thirty-four different prisons in Wisconsin for men and women. Mostly for men but several for women and drug rehabilitation facilities. Several federal prisons were also included.

We used to process all the women at our prison, but that changed, and now they are processed at one of the ladies prisons. One is just west of Fond du Lac, Wisconsin, and it's called Taycheedah Ladies Prison. We were required to house them on several of our units of fifty women each. I can testify, after working on the women's units on several occasions, that they can be as nasty as any mens. This housing for women only lasted a few years. You would not want your kids to hear them or see what they did at times.

Jeffery Dahmer, the serial killer, was a high-priority case. He never came through our prison like all the others. He was sent directly from Milwaukee to our maximum facility in Portage, Wisconsin. This maximum prison would be where he would die also, after being attacked by another inmate. Other high priority prisoners could also be traded to other states because of gang activity or other serious crimes. Some inmates tried to become notorious within the system.

I got to work in the prison I really wanted. It was only fifteen miles from where I lived. It took only a short amount of time to get there. It came in handy, especially in nasty winter weather in Wisconsin.

It was a scary feeling as the steel doors slammed shut behind you the first few days. My age did not mean anything to the group of officers working here. I was now a rookie to all of them even though I was over fifty-two.

I put in thirteen years at the prison, and it was an experience I will never forget. I got into a few fights with inmates that we tried to control. Sometimes it would take several officers to handle just one inmate that wanted to fight. Swearing and spitting at officers was common.

On one occasion in the prison, an inmate decided he was not going to go back to his cell after dinner. They usually marched down the hall to their unit. Instead of going to his unit and eventually to his cell, he decided to wander away down the long hallway. He went down the hall, pounding the walls and doors as he went. He soon pounded on one of the captain's office doors, and the captain came out immediately to see what was going on.

I happened to be coming from the opposite direction when the captain shouted to me, "Jackson! Stop that inmate!"

I confronted the inmate, and he took a swing at me. We were now wrestling and going to the ground. Several other officers were quickly helping me with the unruly inmate. We later could carry pepper spray for inmates like this. We wrestled for several minutes until he was cuffed up and under control. He now got escorted to "the Hole." It was a special maximum area of approximately fifty to seventy inmates who were destined to go to maximum prisons for life or just troublemakers like this guy. He would spend several weeks on this unit for causing trouble.

Inmates did not want to end up here because they no longer got to go outside, go to the dining hall, or have close contact with all the other inmates. They would sit alone in a cell now. They wanted to stay on one of the units.

It was approximately an hour later after the incident in the hall when I was called into the supervisor's offices. Several captains and the shift supervisor were gathered around watching a screen on the desk. Some were laughing. One told me, "Jackson. You have to watch this."

I moved closer as I watched the action on the screen. I knew it was the incident in the hallway earlier. You could clearly see that the hall camera had picked up all the action. At one point, you could see someone fly out of the pile and jump right back into the pile again until the inmate was under control.

The captain said, "That's you, Jackson. That's you flying out of the pile and getting back into it. Fine Job," he said as the others shook my hand. They played it over and over as officers came in to review it. It looked great on film, but I knew how dangerous it could be. I saw several officers get hurt while dealing with inmates over the years. Some cuts, black eyes, and much more. The more serious ones had to take time off or resigned their jobs due to injury.

We sometimes strapped them into special chairs called "restraint chairs." This was because of trouble with the officer or because they got into fights with other inmates. Some would yell obscenities. We never gave out our first names or addresses. Inmates were instructed to call us "Officer Jackson" or "Mr. Jackson" when they addressed us.

No first names were used. Inmates would talk about what obscene things they wanted do to your wife or kids if they found out any personal information about you. Discipline happened all the time. They could lose canteen or, worse, end up in the hole. If the incident was serious enough, they could even receive added time to their sentences.

The hole was the only unit that was loud with inmates. They usually yelled obscenities at officer, especially the female officers. I heard things that I had never heard in fifty years outside the prison. Most of what they wanted to do to us. It was a very loud unit and had usually thirty to fifty men yelling out of their cells through the bars.

The hole was the last stop in this prison because you could be confined in your cell twenty-three out of twenty-four hours. That meant that you got no library, no canteen, no going to the dining room, no recreation in the gym or outside, and no visitors; those privileges were reserved for the other units only and not the hole.

It usually contained fifty to seventy-five inmates and was always very loud. They knew it did not get any worse in our prison unless they were sent to a maximum prison somewhere else in the state. The inmates yelled out obscenities at you as soon as you arrived at the maximum unit for your assignment. Your movement near the inmates had to be monitored carefully. All inmates had to be cuffed and strapped up to even be showered.

It was always advised not to discuss your private life or even where you lived. Inmates would try and call your house if they could find out your number during phone time. Luckily, they were always monitored.

I had many good friends that were fellow officers. Some nasty inmates and some that were ok to be around. There were killers, child molesters, thieves, rapists, and every kind of criminal you could imagine. You always had to be aware of your surroundings and the inmates that were near you. Even the nice ones would gladly try to get you into trouble. I was glad when it was finally over. I felt this was no place for me as I got closer to retirement.

CHAPTER # 14

Retiring At Last

A retirement party was planned, and I knew I would be leaving lots of great fellow officers. I enjoyed working with many men and women over the twelve years.

When I turned sixty-five, I finally retired. They all threw a nice retirement party, and I moved on to the warm climate that I always wanted. Georgia would be our forever home, as my new wife and I would say.

Our kids all got married in Wisconsin, and they have kids of their own. I was blessed with four children and seven grandchildren at the time of this writing,

Leo passed away in 2003 after a long battle with cancer. He left a beautiful family of two sets of twin girls, who have kids now also.

Ferris passed away in California in 1964. It was an auto accident. Dennis and I were not allowed to attend due to a legal agreement Mother had made when she gave us up to the state. We were too young, and other close family may have attended.

The wonderful foster parents both passed away over the years. They were dearly loved people that opened their hearts to Dennis and me both. When attending Mom Saueressigs funeral, I informed everyone in attendance how this family had accepted us with open arms. We'd once yelled, "Take Me! Take me!" in that little room in the children's home, and they did. We were treated as well as any parents could have treated us.

Dennis still lives in Wisconsin and is retired. He's celebrated forty-seven years of marriage and has several grandchildren. We always play golf when we can get together. It is always a great joy. We had to give up playing basketball against each other because it became just too hard for us to do at sixty-five years old. The great memories will always be there.

Karen lives in central Milwaukee. She never married and loves Milwaukee. She also enjoys life in her high-rise apartment, and when I get to Wisconsin, Dennis and I get together with her and go out to dinner. Often talking about those early years.

I now live in Albany, Georgia. Located in the southern part of Georgia, not far from Florida. My wife, Pat, and I enjoy life with my old cars and see the grand kids when we can. The golf course is only about a mile down the road from my house.

It is a funny thing about memories: some are hard to understand, some are great, and life always has surprises. As I retired and settled in Georgia, I grew a beard that I'd never grown before. I was spotted by a gentlemen at the pharmacy who asked if I would be interested in being a Santa at the Albany Mall.

"Who? Me?" I asked.

"Sure," he stated. "You would make a great Santa."

I spent several weeks before Christmas with hundreds of kids and people who wanted to sit on Santa's lap. It was one of the finest things I ever did. A real joy I never expected. My wife so happy that I could do it. She would wait anxiously each time I came home, showing her pictures of lots of kids looking up to Santa.

My four children got married and went on to have children of their own. They have great jobs, and as a father, I could not be prouder of what they are doing bringing up their children.

As I look back, I feel I have had a great life considering the rough start. I look forward to many more years to come. Life is good.

Afterword

It is with great gratitude to my brother Dennis Jackson, sister Karen Jackson, brother Leo Jackson, foster parents Mr. Ervin and Mildred Saueressig, foster brother Russell Saueressig, and foster sister Carol (Saueressig) Raetz that I dedicate this book.

Without their continued love and support, this book could never have been possible.

I wish to thank each of my children, Brian, Bradley, Mellissa, and Michelle, for being the best a father could have. Love you all dearly.

To all the children that have struggled and feel alone in life—I encourage you to lift your heads high and forever fight for a better way. Reach out and continue to love those that are close. Strive to forgive those who make it difficult along the way. Life's trip is ever changing. Whether we are young or old, we must strive to handle it in our own way. Taking the hardships and those fleeting good times in life's everchanging path. Only we can determine our own peace of mind…

—Bruce A. Jackson

Crying Alone

This is the story of a young man that takes you through his struggles from being a boy in a broken family, being torn apart from brothers and sisters, and dealing with being placed in children's homes and foster homes, as well as finding his place in life.

You will be with him through his mischievous years in grammar school, his antics in high school, and how he deals with the hardships and people later in business and in life.

Finally, you will see how he overcomes a rough childhood with very little, becoming successful in life and in business.

CPSIA information can be obtained
at www.ICGtesting.com
Printed in the USA
LVHW061541190521
687633LV00018BA/84/J